John Denver

Anthology

Piano Vocal

Edited by Milton Okun

Associate Music Editor-Dan Fox

ISBN: 0-89524-150-1

D1285738

TABLE OF CONTENTS

ALPHABETICAL LISTING OF SONG TITLES

BIOGRAPHY

John Denver has risen to the pinnacle of every facet of the entertainment industry he has entered. He is the world's leading record seller, a major star of television, one of the biggest concert attractions in the history of show business and, with the release of the Warner Brothers film *O God* he added yet another dimension to a remarkable career—that of a movie star.

The Denver career is one of the great success stories of the entertainment industry. He has an unbroken chain of gold records (often certified gold and even platinum before being shipped to retailers). As a concert attraction in city after city, ticket requests become so great that additional shows are constantly added to keep up with the overwhelming demand.

During the summer of 1975, Denver made his cabaret debut at Harrah's Casino/Hotel in Lake Tahoe. Co-headlining with Frank Sinatra, the event was heralded as nothing short of a historical event in show-business history. In September of '76, the two stars topped that success with an unprecedented three nights at the same showroom appearing together on one stage, and creating near-pandemonium to turn-away crowds.

John Denver is the only star today to establish himself as a major TV personality, not in the usual way, but by a series of top-rated television specials not scheduled at any specific intervals. His specials incorporate both the best in entertainment and the most unusual talent that can possibly be offered, together with a constant concern for excellence. The results have earned Denver outstanding reviews, high ratings and an Emmy Award (*An Evening With John Denver*, best musical-variety special of 1974-75 season). His special, *Rocky Mountain Christmas*, received the highest ratings in the history of the ABC Television Network for a program hosted by a single personality. The *Rocky Mountain Christmas* special was higher than the total of the other two Networks' ratings combined.

In November of 1977, John embarked upon an extensive three-week concert tour of Australia and New Zealand and also taped his first 90-minute television special, a tour de force not only in talent but also an enormous undertaking, as it was filmed entirely on location throughout the continent of Australia.

John Denver is the recipient of the Country Music Association (CMA) highest award, *Entertainer of the Year,* as well as winning *Song of the Year* for *Back Home Again.*

John Denver's popularity encompasses a complete cross-section of the music-listening audience. He is probably the only artist who consistently registers strong response on the National Charts, the Country Music Charts and the Easy Listening Charts.

From State Fair Grounds to posh nightclubs, Denver's compositions have been performed by a diverse roster of stars: Frank Sinatra, Peggy Lee, Julie Andrews, Arthur Fiedler, Andre Kostelanetz, Carol Burnett, Loretta Lynn, Conway Twitty, Lawrence Welk, The Osmond Brothers, Vikki Carr, Eddy Arnold, Percy Faith, Englebert Humperdinck, Olivia Newton-John, Ray Coniff, Lynn Anderson, Bobby Vinton, Mantovani, Brenda Lee and a score of others. Because of his own status as the world's top-selling recording artist, his television specials and film scores, his sell-out concerts and because of the many other artists who record and perform his songs, John Denver is today the world's most listened-to modern composer.

Denver has been singing and writing about the beauties of nature and of romanticism for a long time. He sings from the perspective of a *country boy,* reflecting on the joys of rural living and, since he has lived the experiences, he is certainly a qualified spokesman.

John Denver's songs are celebrations of trees and flowers, the Rocky Mountains, blue skies, the woman he loves—all that is beautiful and good on this earth. There is an ever-present regard for the state of Man and the human condition. Always there, in lyric and expression, is a positive, optimistic stance on Man's potential for better things.

Born Henry John Deutchendorf on New Year's Eve 1943, in Roswell, New Mexico, John grew up in an Air Force family. His formal education was nomadic, with towns from Kansas to California now claiming him as a hometown boy.

In college at Texas Tech, he studied architecture, and like most young men at the time, folk music deeply affected him. He knew he could sing and California was where it was at for a burgeoning *folky.* A 1955 Chevy got him there.

John secured a job in Los Angeles as a draftsman. At night he sang in the coffee houses and eventually cut some demonstration records. He also changed his name to John Denver, taking his new last name from his favorite city.

The demo records proved a vehicle for mobility, in this case Los Angeles to New York. John was requested to come East to audition as Chad Mitchell's replacement in the extremely-popular Chad Mitchell Trio. There were close to 250 candidates for the job but he got it.

After two-and-a-half years as lead singer for the group, Denver decided to take a whack at being a single performer. Shortly thereafter he came into national prominence, via an ironic route.

His composition, *Leaving On A Jet Plane,* was in his first album *Rhymes and Reasons.* It was not an immediate success until Peter, Paul and Mary recorded the song as a single and it swept the country. He ran second with his own version of the song but he finally had that elusive hit.

He fast became a major attraction on the college concert circuit, while methodically building a reputation as a solid recording artist. Four RCA albums later, he had a million-seller in *Take Me Home, Country Roads,* written by Denver in collaboration with Bill Danoff and Taffy Nivert. The song came from the LP, *Poems, Prayers and Promises,* also a gold album in sales.

From the Universal Ampitheatre in Los Angeles (where Denver created a sensation and set a house record by selling out seven days' performance in 24 hours) to New York's legendary Carnegie Hall, the people came in droves to see and hear John Denver. In the last three years, he has appeared in 10 sell-out concert tours, many of which sold out by a mere mention on a local radio station. In the summer of '76, he donated the proceeds from his regularly-scheduled series of five concerts in Los Angeles to various institutions and charities in and around the area. The event was termed *The John Denver Summer Festival of Charities.*

Rocky Mountain High, released in 1972, is still one of Denver's banner LP's with close to two-and-a-half million in sales. He followed that one with *Farewell, Andromeda,* another bonanza which featured such Denver compositions as *I'd Rather Be a Cowboy, Rocky Mountain Suite* and the title song, *Farewell, Andromeda.*

Denver continued his hit string with what has become one of the biggest-selling records in the industry's history, *John Denver's Greatest Hits.* The album, which still continues to rank among the nation's best-selling records, has been high on the charts for four years with no decline in sight.

Despite his intensive personal-appearance tours, John does not like to travel. John and his wife, Annie, live in Aspen, Colorado. She does not always accompany him on his tours, preferring to stay home. The Denver family would be totally rooted if it were not for the demands of show business. His song, *Goodbye Again,* from the *Rocky Mountain High* LP, best explains his negative feelings about being away from his wife and home.

The Denvers enjoy their life in Aspen. There is time to pursue his favorite sport, skiing. He paints, is a do-it-yourselfer around the house, rides horses and his favorite motorcycle, and keeps an active interest in local, national and world affairs from his home base. His songs clearly indicate a concern for humanity. They also present his great love for nature that, at his home in the Rocky Mountains, is fully satisfied.

His tremendous success on his first *John Denver Show* in March, 1974 was not an overnight happening. John hosted the pilot for NBC-TV's *Midnight Special* in 1972. In January, 1973, John narrated and starred in the television film, *Bighorn,* an ecology-oriented special on the endangered Rocky Mountain Big Horn sheep.

He starred in a series of specials for the BBC in London, and, as an indication of his wide audience appeal, has guest-hosted the *Tonight* show on several occasions in Johnny Carson's absence.

For the last decade, John has become known not only for his many hit songs but also for his involvement in many issues affecting mankind and the world we live in. He has been a vocal proponent of protecting the environment, saving the whales, space exploration, and the development of innovative approaches to energy usage. In 1978, John was named by President Carter to serve as a member of the Presidential Commission on World Hunger.

In 1976, John founded The Windstar Foundation, which supports the Windstar Project. Located in Snowmass, Colorado, Windstar is a research and education center devoted to developing workable models for scientific and technological progress which retain a sense of harmony among people working together, between mankind and the physical environment, and between our everyday concerns and our own spirituality.

John Denver has reached the pinnacle of his profession through pure talent and straight talk. There are no added frills, glitter and makeup, or firework theatrics at a Denver show—just honest, basic communication on things that are important to all of us. John's ballads ask us to open our hearts and minds to all that is good and beautiful around us.

PERFORMANCE NOTES

Since the turbulent 60's, the songs of John Denver have been an important part of the American music scene. This anthology contains all his hits since the earliest made famous by Peter, Paul and Mary, *Leaving On A Jet Plane* and *For Baby*, through the exquisite *Annie's Song* and *Take Me Home, Country Roads* to his very latest, *Some Days Are Diamonds*.

The arrangements in this collection are designed to be enjoyed by the average non-professional player, while yielding a thoroughly professional sounding performance.

Consider the vocal line:

It is always the highest note in the right hand of the piano, and is almost always stemmed up. Each line captures John's forceful, yet subtle, country-folk inflections. Take special note of the smaller sized cue notes; they represent the slides, grace notes and other embellishments so beloved of country singers. By engraving them in a contrasting size, we make it easy for the pianist to simplify his part by leaving out these important, but not crucial, embellishments.

Speaking of pianists, they too will be delighted with this anthology. Their parts are easy to play and lie "under the hand," yet yield an authentic sounding performance. It may be useful here to remind players that country music generally has a swing feeling, and that 8th notes are played like ♪³♪ rather than the exactly even 8th note feeling in rock and classical music.

As John Denver is such a fine accompanist of his own music on the guitar we have designed these arrangements to reproduce as much as possible his own styles and chord progressions. Look at his famous love song *My Sweet Lady* (p.60) for example. Note the care the arranger has taken to give you the exact form of each chord just as John plays it. Not just any Dmaj7 is the first chord, but the particular form of that chord that will yield the best sounding and logical progression.

We have also taken care to indicate special tunings when used, for example, the D tuning on *My Sweet Lady* and *Poems, Prayers and Promises*, and in placing the capo when appropriate. Look at *Aspenglow* (p.30). The capo is used not because the song isn't playable in the written key, but because placing it at the 5th fret makes the chords sound higher and more delicate in keeping with the subject matter of the song. Using the capo also avoids awkward keys such as Ab (capo up 1 fret from G), Eb (capo up 1 fret from D) and so on.

We think that John Denver's millions of fans will like this book for its completeness, the care with which it has been assembled, and especially for the dozens of great songs, without which the last ten or fifteen years of the American music scene would have been inconceivable.

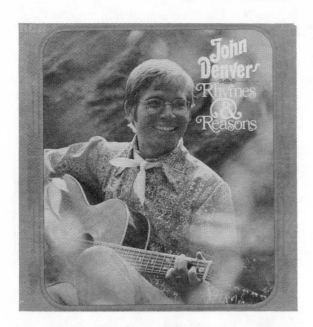

From the album
RHYMES AND REASONS

Release date: 1969

LEAVING ON A JET PLANE, was initially called *Oh Babe I Hate To Go.* Milt Okun is responsible for that title change—I shall be forever grateful to him. *Leaving On A Jet Plane* resulted from my way of life at that time. I was working with The Mitchell Trio and lived on the road. Either I stayed where the last concert was or I'd go to the next concert city a bit early. I didn't have a home. I didn't have a place to call my own. I didn't have a room and clothes and records piled someplace. Everything was in storage in California and I lived out of suitcases on the road-always leaving on a jet plane. I didn't have anyone to sing that song to. That's why so much of the song has to do with the description of leaving someone. I wished I had someone I could leave—a home and a place that I could leave, knowing that I would be returning. There was nothing solid for me in my relationships, either with my family or with friends, and the song is a picture of how I wanted it to be as opposed to the way it was.

RHYMES AND REASONS is, I think, one of the best songs I've ever written. I wrote the song-or started it at least—in the shower one morning. It comes from a very real and consistent thought that the children and the flowers are my sisters and my brothers. I do not feel separate from any aspect or form of life. I feel part of it, and bound to it, and the way I expressed the feeling was to use the phrase, "the children and the flowers." There is a brotherhood there, and a sisterhood. It's funny to me that even before the time of women's liberation there was a desire to uphold that concept. The song is basically autobiographical. It's not one of those songs where I've described someone who has a job to do in the world. I'm describing who that person is—the song is about me. I intend to lead people to the mountains; I intend to lead them back to the earth, back to the spirit. Songs like *Rhymes And Reasons* are a way of doing that for me.

DAY DREAMS At the time *Day Dreams* was written, I was starting to spend more time writing songs and expressing myself. Many of the songs on the early albums were exercises in trying to put a thought down and make it complete—musically giving it a beginning, an ending, and something to relate to. In *Day Dreams* I can picture this guy having broken up with the lady he cared for, and finding himself daydreaming about her and their relationship, and wishing it was still going on—wishing he could recreate it, which of course is impossible.

Rhymes And Reasons

Words and Music by
John Denver

Day Dreams

Words and Music by
John Denver

* *Note special tuning for guitar: 6th string=C, 5th string=G, 4th string=C, 3rd string=F, 2nd string=A, 1st string=D.*

Circus

Words and Music by
Michael Johnson, John Denver and Laurie Kuehn

Leaving On A Jet Plane

Words and Music by
John Denver

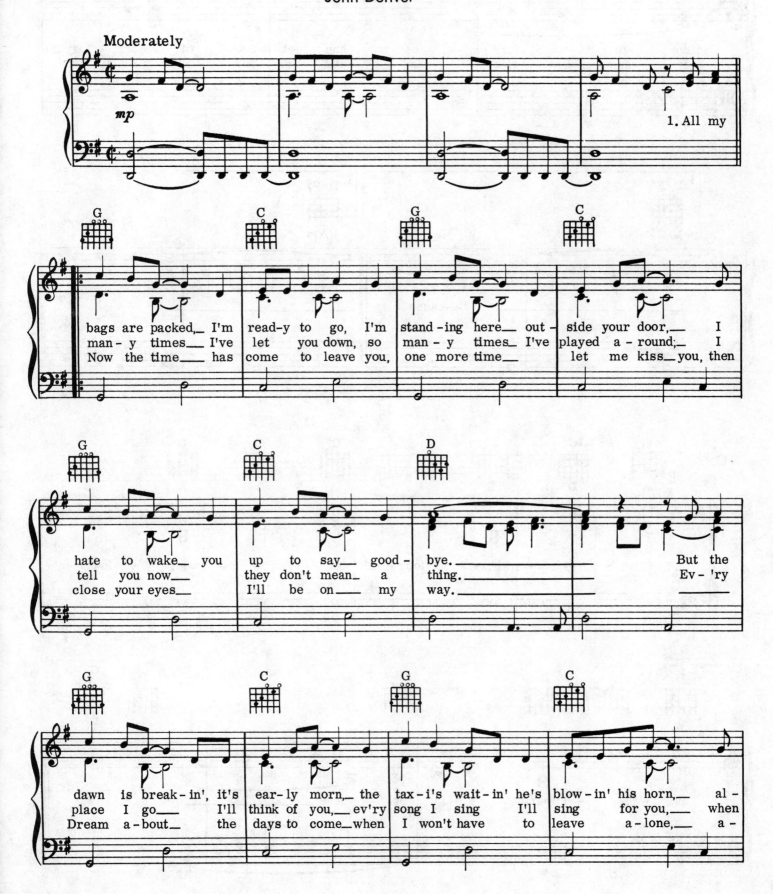

From the album
TAKE ME TO TOMORROW

Release date: 1970

TAKE ME TO TOMORROW is a song of dissatisfaction about
the way I saw things around me. I could sing that song just as easily today as I did back then. I wanted a hard driving song that expressed frustration and anger—a protest song. I haven't written very many of those, but my feelings at the time were that I was getting tired of the world we live in, at least the world that we have made as human beings. It's a world in constant conflict, with people working not for each other, but against each other, trying to separate themselves from each other—to make life not work. You know, I'm ready for tomorrow. I have a vision of tomorrow out there working, a world that works, and that's where I want to be. Take me to tomorrow, take me there today. I've had my fill of sorrow and living this way. Take me to tomorrow, that's where I'd like to be. The day after tomorrow is waiting for me.

FOLLOW ME is one of my very favorite songs, the second of what I call my
Jet Plane Trilogy. Once again, it has to do with being on the road, leaving the person you care for and going off on your own. This time, I had found someone that I wanted with me all the time. We just couldn't afford to do that, though. I found myself out on the road alone, trying to make enough money for us to live as a family, and not able to have what I wanted most: the companionship, the being there of Annie.

ASPENGLOW was written in a little town that I love in the Rocky
Mountains. The townspeople have a celebration every year called Winterskol, and each year it has a theme. The first winter I was working in Aspen, the theme was Aspenglow. They talk about "taking on an Aspenglow," the connotation being that somehow just living here brings on a glow that shows the effect of this little town on your life. Being up here in the mountains, living the way we do up here does enhance your life. You come here even now and people look different. Their faces are shiny, they're healthy, they're outdoor people. There's a sense of community and being with one another, having lived through some hard winter storms, cold nights on the mountain, thunderstorms and brush fires. So, an Aspenglow is what I describe in the song. Aspenglow is a sense of family, of living here, of being able to appreciate the little subtleties which are so often missed; sunlight through the pine, the warmth of winter wine, sitting down and having a glass of wine with someone at a picnic on the side of a mountain. All of a sudden that little sharing of the cup can mean a whole lot of things. That's what you try to do with a song—to take the whole world of experience and put it in a three minute song.

ISABEL is a fantasy—another exercise in taking an idea and writing a song about it. I wanted to be as flowery and poetic as possible in the language of describing a dream—a real dream. I wanted to put the notion out there without ever saying it is a dream. The song is a dream about a person.

ANTHEM-REVELATION is a song of celebration—a celebration of every new day, every new beginning and every new moment. It's opportunity that's always there, that always needs to be created. Even at its darkest and worst moments, life is full of potential, full of opportunity, and full of joy.

STICKY SUMMER WEATHER I don't know if you've ever been in Washington, D.C. or Philadelphia or places like that in the summer, but, it gets incredibly hot and humid. When you can't sleep at night and you're all by yourself, your mind starts dancing around with ideas and notions. I feel very fortunate in that I can pick up my guitar and play with the experience. . .and maybe a song comes through. *Sticky Summer Weather* is like that. Instead of being hot and uncomfortable, you'd really like to be somewhere like the desert after a rainstorm. Rainbows appear over the mountains, and the whole world is clean, fresh and sweet again.

Take Me To Tomorrow

Words and Music by
John Denver

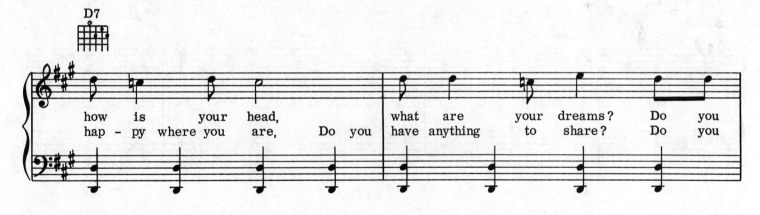

Aspenglow

Words and Music by
John Denver

See the sun-light through the pine,
As the win-ter days un-fold

taste the warm of win-ter wine,
hearts grow warm-er with the cold,

dream of soft-ly fall-ing snow,
peace of mind is all you know,

win-ter sköl,

As-pen-glow.

As-pen is a life to live,

see how much there is to give,

Follow Me

Words and Music by
John Denver

*Guitarists: Tune lowest string to D.

Anthem-Revelation

Words and Music by
John Denver

March tempo

See the sun-rise, _____ o-pen up your eyes, _____ to-day is the ver-y first day. _____ Watch the morn-ing come, _____ Now the night is gone, _____ Yes-ter-day's_ so ver-y far a-way. _____

Sticky Summer Weather

Words and Music by
John Denver

Isabel

Words and Music by
John Denver

Lyrics:

Is-a-bel is wait-ing in a room of man-y shad-ows,____ Her
eyes like flash-ing dia-monds shin-ing bright-ly from the sea, Her
hair in silk-en tress-es like the robe a-round her shoul-der hid-ing
tan-ta-liz-ing treas-ures____ that the sun has nev-er seen.

wraps her arms a- round me and she sighs,_____ And she
whis-pers as she sad-ly slips a- way,_____ Then she

sings to me in si- lence with her eyes,_____ and her
smiles be-cause there's noth-ing left to say,_____ and she

hair up-on my pil-low_____ com-forts me._____
takes with her the sad-ness_____ and the song._____

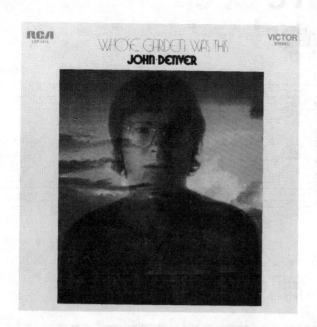

From the album
WHOSE GARDEN WAS THIS

Release date: 1970

SAIL AWAY HOME was written the day after Kent State, and deals with the dissatisfaction of our young people regarding a war they didn't understand or want to be a part of. To have them take a stand against fighting and getting shot down was incredible. Take me away from this place, give me the chance to make a better world. I wasn't just saying it for me—I hope I was saying it for those people who stood in the midst of that gunfire, the people who died there.

I WISH I COULD HAVE BEEN THERE (Woodstock)

is an expression of a special event involving half a million people, from someone who was there spiritually but would have loved to have been there physically.

SWEET, SWEET LIFE The album *Whose Garden Was This* is pretty much a joyless album. I tried to bring it back at the end with the song *Sweet, Sweet Life*. I felt as if I'd reached the end of my tether. As depressed as I was and as heavy as everything felt to me (life was not worth living), my absolute prayerful and agonizing cry was to live. Give me one more chance. Let me find once again the joy and the celebration.

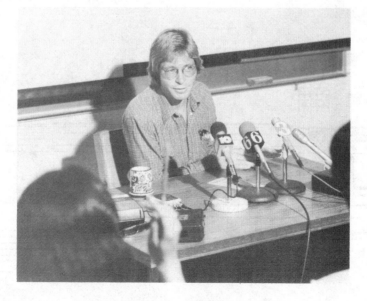

I Wish I Could Have Been There
(Woodstock)

Words and Music by
John Denver

sing as the rhy-thm and the words came float-ing by. I

wish I could have been there in the star - light when the coun-try-side was qui-et once a-

gain, and the mu-sic and the mak-ers, the po-ets and the sing-ers,

Repeat and fade

and the chil-dren of the flow-ers had all gone.

47

Sail Away Home

Words and Music by
John Denver

you don't know.____
like to be.____

Dream a - way,
Don't you know

it seems so   wrong,____   yeah,____

Don't you know   it's gone on too__   long.____

I can't take the   guns an-y-more,   I can't take the

Sweet, Sweet Life

Words and Music by
John Denver

From the album
POEMS, PRAYERS & PROMISES

Release date: 1971

TAKE ME HOME, COUNTRY ROADS

The first album that had great success for me was an album called *Poems, Prayers & Promises,* and the song that really made that album a success is one that I wrote with two friends, Bill and Taffy Danoff, from Starland Vocal Band. I met them at a place called The Cellar Door in Washington, D.C. when I was working with the Mitchell Trio and started performing on my own. I had an opportunity to have my first headline show at the Cellar Door, and they asked me who I wanted for an opening act. I asked about having Bill and Taffy there. They did come and open the shows for me. The first night we were together we went back to their place after closing, just to visit, see what was going on and enjoy being together. We had a bunch of songs we wanted to show each other. One of the songs was one they had started and were unable to complete. It was a song called *Take Me Home, Country Roads.* In the wee hours of the morning, sometime between Christmas and New Year's Eve, in their basement apartment in Washington, D.C., we wrote *Take Me Home, Country Roads.* It became my first #1 record and million seller. It's really a great song, you know—Almost heaven, West Virginia.

POEMS, PRAYERS AND PROMISES is another of my

very favorite songs. It's a song that comes from a very mellow space of family and friends; sitting around enjoying each other and enjoying life in a way that has no time attached to it—no urgency and no frustration. It's a peaceful time of being together and sharing the things that are on your mind in a very positive kind of way.

MY SWEET LADY is an absolute love song. It has to do with the

discovery that you have a true and deep and meaningful love. 'I am incredibly in love with you and I want to be with you. So, the tears and the sadness there—you know, let me kiss those away. Let me profess once again that I am here with you.' *My Sweet Lady* seems to be one of the most popular of my songs for lovers.

WOODEN INDIAN is another strong expression of frustration and dis-

satisfaction. It's unusual for me to be moved to write something out of desperation. In my travels across the United States performing and singing for people, I became aware of this one aspect of our society and of our heritage that we have not treated very well—the American Indian. Within my own viewpoint, there is a better way for them to achieve the things they're trying to achieve, and I totally support what they're going for, though I don't often find it very easy to support the way they're doing it. At the same time I wanted to express my experience of their feelings. That's *Wooden Indian.* I swear by my grandfather's father, we shall rise again.

SUNSHINE ON MY SHOULDERS has an interesting

background. There was a movie being made at that time that I was asked to write a song for. It had to do with two people who were going to die, and they knew they were going to die, so this is how they spent their last day together. In a lot of the things they did, they were celebrating; enjoying being with each other and making love, and going to the beach and laughing and dancing in the waves. And yet there was this overriding sense of sadness through it all. The scene *Sunshine* was written for was the scene where they were laughing and dancing in the water. I wrote the song in Minnesota at the time I call late winter, early spring. It was a dreary day, gray and slushy. The snow was melting and it's too cold to go outside and have fun, and if you do, you get all sloppy and dirty, but God, you're ready for spring. You want to get outdoors again and you're waiting for that sun and looking for it. So, in that very melancholy frame of mind I wrote *Sunshine On My Shoulders.*

Poems, Prayers And Promises

Words and Music by
John Denver

* Guitarists: Tune lowest string to D.

know I'm gon-na hate to see it end.
turns me on to think of grow-ing old. For I've

seen a lot of sun - shine,
tho' my life's been good to me, there's still so much to do, so

spent a night or two all on my own, I've
man - y things my mind has nev-er known, I'd

known my la - dy's pleas - ures, I'd
like to raise a fam - 'ly, I'd like to sail a - way, and

had my-self some friends,
like to sail a - way, and

spent a time or two___ in my own home.___
dance a-cross the moun-tains on the moon.___

I

have to say it now___ it's been a good___ life all___ in all, it's real-ly fine___

___ to have the chance___ to hang a-round,___ and lie there by the fire___ and

watch the eve-ning tire,___ while all___ my friends and my old la-dy sit and

My Sweet Lady

Words and Music by
John Denver

Moderately

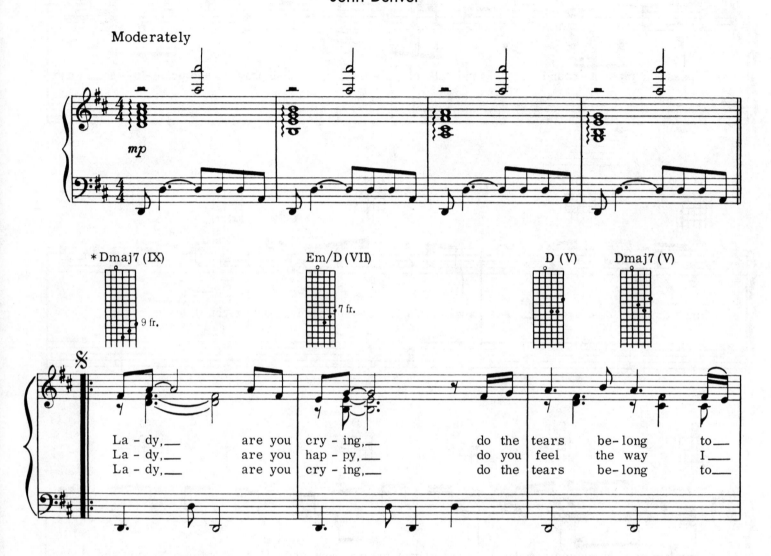

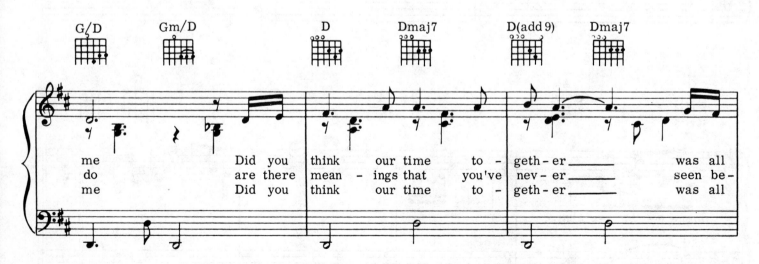

Lady,___ are you cry-ing,___ do the tears be-long to___
Lady,___ are you hap-py,___ do you feel the way I___
La-dy,___ are you cry-ing,___ do the tears be-long to___

me   Did you think our time to-geth-er___ was all
do   are there mean-ings that you've nev-er___ seen be-
me   Did you think our time to-geth-er___ was all

* Guitarists: Tune lowest string to D.

Take Me Home, Country Roads

Words and Music by
Bill Danoff, Taffy Nivert and John Denver

young - er than the moun - tains___ grow - in' like a breeze.
mist - y taste of moon - shine,___ tear - drop in my eye.

Coun - try Roads,___ take__ me home___ to the

place___ I be - long:___ West Vir - gin - ia,___

moun - tain mom - ma,___ Take__ me home,___ Coun - try

Roads.___ All my I hear her voice, in the

Wooden Indian

**Words and Music by
John Denver**

Moderately bright

Em * *(throughout)*

I was a red man I was proud I was strong; you were the white man and you
I was a red man in my passing made no sound; you were the white man and you
I was a red man I was proud I was strong; you were the white man and you

took a - way my__ home. Now I am a wood-en In - di - an paint - ed
drove me in the__ ground. Now I am a wood-en In - di - an stand - ing
took a - way my__ home. Now I am a wood-en In - di - an stand - ing

* Guitarists: Use hammer on effect on the 5th string from the 5th fret to the 7th fret. This is used throughout the intro and the first halves of the verses. On the 2nd halves of the verses, simply hammer on the normal Em chord.

dreams in-side my__ head,
si – lent in the__ rain,   I
si – lent in the__ rain,   I

'times the way you bring__ me down make me
swear by my grand-fa – ther's fa-ther
swear by my grand-fa – ther's fa-ther

wish that I was__ dead!⟩
we're gonna rise a – gain!⟩
we're gonna rise a – gain!⟩

Guitar: ⑤ 7 fr.------------------- 5 fr.-------- 2 fr. etc.

Na   na   na na na na

2nd time, 8va higher

na   na   na na na na na   na   na   na na na na na na na   na na na na na.

1. 2.   **3.**

Ay,

Gospel Changes

Words and Music by
Jack Williams

* Guitarists: Tune lowest string to D.

I Guess He'd Rather Be In Colorado

Words and Music by
Bill Danoff and Taffy Nivert

Easy tempo

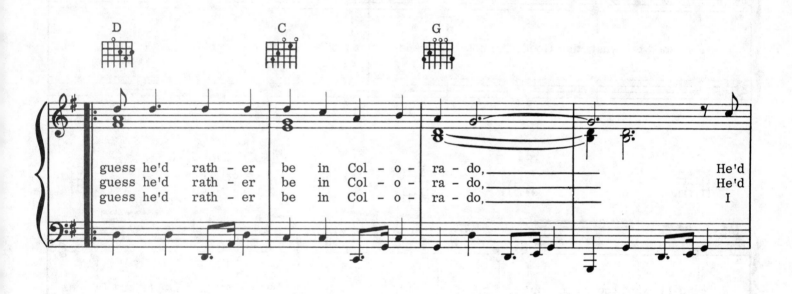

guess he'd rath – er be in Col – o – ra – do,_____ He'd
guess he'd rath – er be in Col – o – ra – do,_____ He'd
guess he'd rath – er be in Col – o – ra – do,_____ I

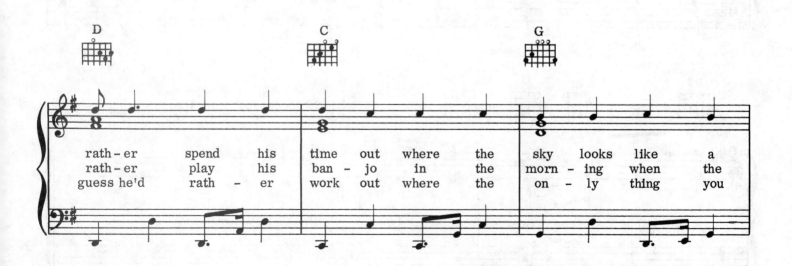

rath – er spend his time out where the sky looks like a
rath – er play his ban – jo in the morn – ing when the
guess he'd rath – er work out where the on – ly thing you

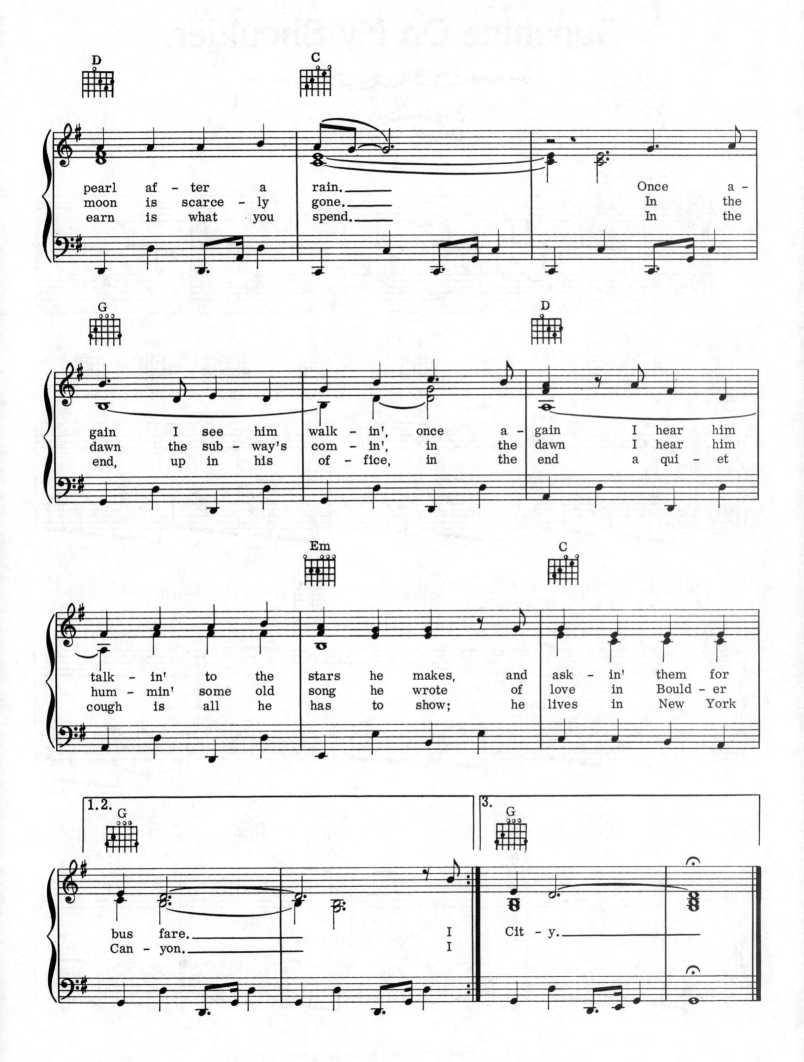

Sunshine On My Shoulders

Words by John Denver
Music by John Denver, Mike Taylor and Dick Kniss

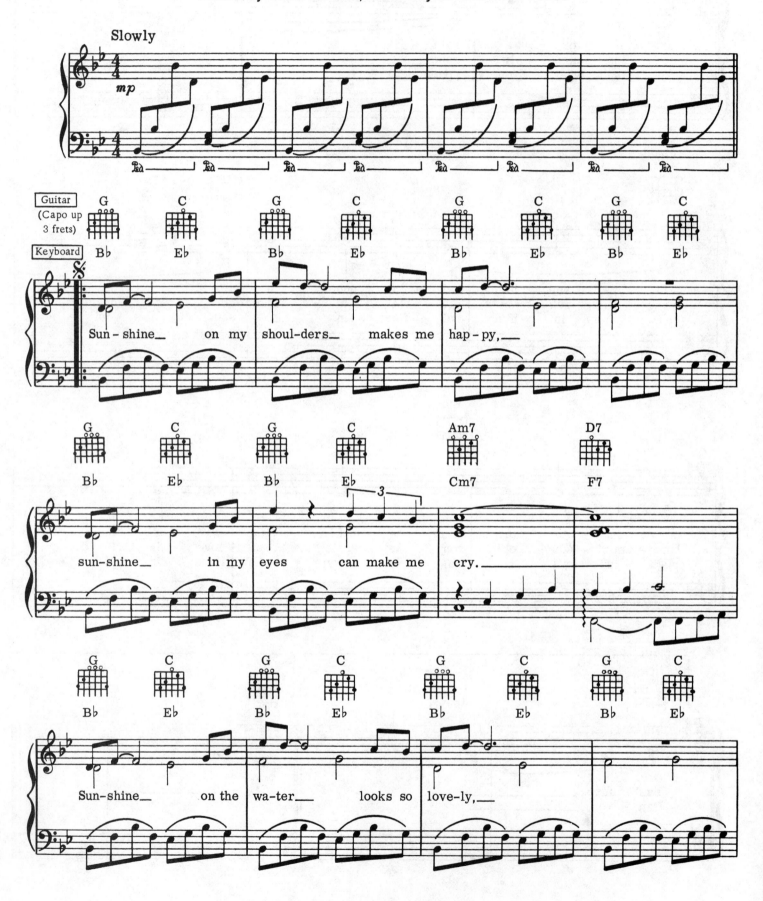

From the album
AERIE

Release date: Spring 1972

THE EAGLE AND THE HAWK
was written for a television show that I did with my old friend Rogert Riger. The show starred Nell Newman, the daughter of Joanne and Paul Newman, and another old friend Morley Nelson. Morley lives in Boise, Idaho and knows more about birds of prey than any man in the world. The song came as a result of his work with these birds, his concern for them. He would mend their broken wings, take care of the young if the parents had not returned to the nest and he did a lot of research on how to keep eagles safe when they build their nests on high power line structures. I realized that Morley's just a wonderful man, and to this day the song is one of my favorites. It's a very powerful song in a very positive way. I have only recently been able to appreciate what this song was meant for, having to do with dancing and flying with the mountains the way the eagles do. Oh, I love to fly like an eagle.

STARWOOD IN ASPEN
was written for a place where I was going to make my aerie; a place that felt like home to Annie and me. It's a beautiful place on the side of a mountain near Aspen, Colorado. The first time we were there, we knew that it was our home. Without ever having lived there, or having spent time there, I was able to create in my mind what I initially wanted to tell people about: How far it was to Los Angeles, where I started making music. It was the song I used to open my concerts for a long time—to tell people this is where I come from, I'm happy to be here, and it's still a long way from this place to Denver, a long time to hang in the sky, a long way home. It's not really a long way home—home is wherever you are.

TOOLS
The song is the story. We lived in a little apartment building in Minnesota. One day, the caretaker showed us a nest of four baby rabbits he had found. The mother never returned and three of the rabbits died. We took the fourth one, *Tools*, and cared for him to the best of our ability. After a few days he passed on too and I wrote a song about it.

The Eagle And The Hawk

Words by John Denver
Music by John Denver and Mike Taylor

blood on my_ feath-ers, but time is still turn-ing they soon will be dry._____ And

all those who see me and all who be-lieve in me share in the free-dom I

feel when I fly._____

Come dance with the west wind and touch on the moun-tain tops,

sail o'er the can - yons and up to the stars, And reach for the heav - ens and hope for the fu - ture and all that we can be and not what we are.

Twice as fast

Starwood In Aspen

Words and Music by
John Denver

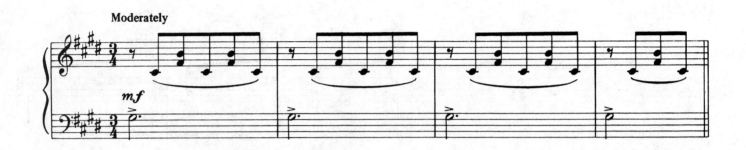

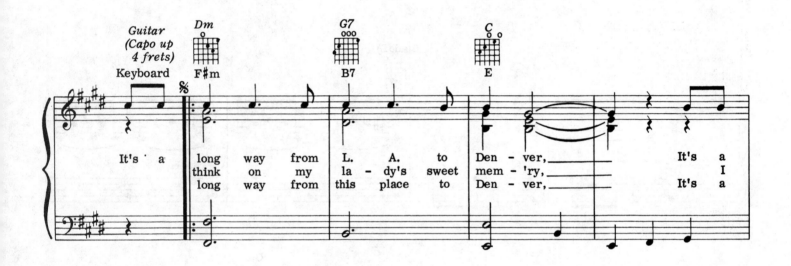

It's a long way from L. A. to Den - ver, It's a
think on my la - dy's sweet mem - 'ry, I
long way from this place to Den - ver, It's a

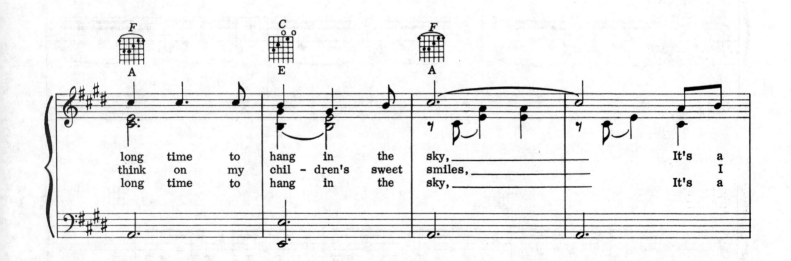

long time to hang in the sky, It's a
think on my chil - dren's sweet smiles, I
long time to hang in the sky, It's a

Friends With You

Words and Music by
Bill Danoff and Taffy Nivert

Tools

Words and Music by
John Denver

Tools was a ba-by rab - bit, he was a friend of mine,___ His

D.C. and fade

From the album
ROCKY MOUNTAIN HIGH

Release date: Fall 1972

FOR BABY (FOR BOBBIE) is actually the first song that I ever

wrote. It was first recorded on an album with the Mitchell Trio, and then I included it on the *Rocky Mountain High* album. It was written for a girl named Bobbie Wargo, who I was in love with once upon a time when I was first starting out in the world with my music and trying to make it as a performer. The song fits her well and is a very accurate representation of the shape and form of our love at the time—all that it was, and all that it wasn't. Mary Travers (of Peter, Paul and Mary) then expanded the song and made it a love song for her daughter. It made the song so much more for me and for everybody else. It's great that a song can be appreciated on different levels like that. So, it's for Bobbie—a love song between a man and a woman (not quite yet a man and a woman), and For Baby—a love song from a woman to her newborn child. It's wonderful.

GOODBYE AGAIN is the third of what I called earlier, The Jet Plane

Trilogy. Annie and I were living in Aspen and we were in a much better position to afford her traveling with me when she wanted to, but, Annie doesn't much like to travel. She doesn't like the one-night stands and would rather be at home with our family and friends. So, there's a constant on-going process of goodbye again for us. In recent years it has gotten easier, but it's still difficult. It's not easy to accept. It's a difficult thing to work within a relationship and there's pain involved. You know, it's hard to say goodbye again sometimes.

ROCKY MOUNTAIN HIGH, the title song of the album, was

written after we had moved to the Rocky Mountains. We were living there, starting to go camping, and everything that I had longed for all my life was now here and around me. I found some new friends and lost a friend—killed on my motorcycle when he and his wife were visiting us over one weekend. Within that framework there was also a big controversy in Colorado—working to get the Winter Olympics of 1972 in Colorado. The feeling was that what they were going to do, the money that was going to be spent and the scars that would be made were going to support something that most probably would never be used again. The combination of all these things inspired me to write *Rocky Mountain High.*

SEASON SUITE

was written for a film done back in Minnesota about the seasons. I sat down and spent some time with each of the four seasons in my mind and put together the way I held them—what they reflected for me. I had the chance to add that fifth season, *Late Winter, Early Spring (When Everybody Goes To Mexico)*. It's the time when the snow is melting, the whole world is muddy and people are taking a break, going off on some trip to relax in the sun. I did all the music with Dick Kniss and Mike Taylor, my accompanists at the time. We gave the song a link and a form, without it having a melody. Then Mike Taylor, an incredible guitar player, spent a whole day in the studio trying to play through the whole song, and he couldn't do it. At the end of the day, we had five separate tracks and there was no cohesiveness or thread to it. Something would start and it wouldn't end, and then it would all fall apart. Finally, Kris O'Connor and I sat down, and as we kept listening to each of the tracks, we found a thread and a melody line, and a way the song built and then retarded. It was the mix that made the record and it came to be a beautiful piece of music. Lee Holdridge's version with the orchestra is one of the loveliest things I've ever heard. This is an example of a whole lot of people working together to get one thing to happen. I'm very grateful to Mike Taylor for his guitar playing, and to Kris, Milt and our engineer, Ray Hall, for persevering and getting it done.

HARD LIFE, HARD TIMES (Prisoners)

Again, another one of those very few songs that was hard and angry. In this case, it was bitter more than anything else. The song describes a situation involving two people. One, the man who's a prisoner and unable to be home. He communicates through letters to his woman who is far from him, with a newborn baby the father has never even seen. The child doesn't know the father and she gets these letters which start to mean less and less. Realizing she may never see him again, she is trying to maintain stability by working—to keep herself occupied and to support herself and her child and not able to really enjoy life. There are too many restraints. So, the song is called *Hard Life, Hard Times (Prisoners)*. I always felt it was a very powerful song.

For Baby (For Bobbie)

Words and Music by
John Denver

love you more than an - y - bod - y can.
flec - tion of the love_____ in your eyes.

And the wind will whis - per your name to me,
And I'll sing you the songs of the rain - bow,

The

Lit - tle birds_ will sing a - long_ in time,_____
whis - per of_____ the joy_____ that_ is mine,_____

The leaves will bow down when

you walk by And morn - ing bells will chime.

Goodbye Again

Words and Music by
John Denver

Slowly, but with a double-time feeling

It's five o-clock this morn-ing and the sun is on the rise There's
(2.) seems a shame to leave you now the days are soft and warm I
(4.) if your hours are emp-ty now who am I to blame You

frost-ing on the win-dow pane and sor-row in your eyes The stars are fad-ing qui-et-ly the
long to lay me down a-gain and hold you in my arms I long to kiss the tears a-way and
think if I were al-ways here our love would be the same As it is the time we have is

night is near-ly gone And so you turn a-way from me and
give you back your smile But oth-er voic-es beck-on me
worth the time a-lone And ly-ing by your side the great-est

tears be-gin to come. And it's
for a lit-tle while. It's good-bye a-gain, I'm sor-ry to be leav-ing you, Good-
peace I've ev-er known. And it's

Rocky Mountain High

Words and Music by
John Denver and Mike Taylor

*Guitarists: Tune low E down to D.

But the string's al-read-y bro - ken and he
His sight has turned in - side him-self to
Why they try to tear the moun - tains down to

does-n't real-ly care, it keeps chang - in' fast and
try and un-der-stand more peo - ple of a
bring in a cou-ple more the se - ren-i-ty of a

it don't last for long.
clear blue moun-tain lake.
scars up - on the land.

But the
And the
And the

Col - o - ra - do Rock - y Moun-tain high, I've

Hard Life, Hard Times
(Prisoners)

Words and Music by
John Denver

town   five and dime,__ an - y - thing__ at all__ to help her   pass the time.__

__ Her ma-ma keeps the ba - by__ and

grand-pa ram-bles on __ a-bout the good times __ a-play-in' in his   mind.__

It's a hard __ life liv-in' when you're lone - ly,__ it's a long __

night sleep-in' a-lone, __ It's a hard __ time wait-ing for to-mor-

row, __ it's a long, __ long __ way home. __

Jo-sie spends __ the eve-ning __ with the peo - ple on the pa - ges of the pa-

per back_ she pickedup at the store._ Well,

some-times it's the T._ V._ she'll try to write a let - ter, Wo!_

they don't come too of - ten an - y - more._ It's a hard_

_ life liv - in' when you're lone - ly,_ it's a long_

night sleep-in' a-lone,____ It's a hard____

time wait-ing for to - mor - row,____ it's a long,____

long____ way home.____

I stare at the gray_walls be-fore____

me ___ I see ___ her face in the dawn. ___ I

try to im-ag - ine our ba - by, ___ I wish they would let ___ me go home. ___

___ I wish they would let ___ me go home. ___

(group) I

wish they would let me go home,

It's a hard ___ life liv - in' when you're lone- I

home,
wish they would let me go home,
bring __ me and __ the oth - er boys
I

home,
wish they would let me go home.
bring __ me and __ the oth - er boys

Tacet
home.

Repeat and fade

Ped.

Repeat and fade
mp

Summer

Words and Music by
John Denver, Mike Taylor and Dick Kniss

To Coda

I love the life a-round me, a part of ev-'ry-thing is here in me.

Rid-ing on the tap-es-try of all there is to see, so man-y ways and oh so man-y things. Re-joic-ing in the dif-f'renc-es there's

no one just like me   yet as   dif-f'rent as: we are   we're still the same.

D. S. al Coda 𝄋

And oh,

Coda

me.   A part

of ev - 'ry-thing   is here   in   me   A part   of ev-

- 'ry - thing   is here   in   me.

Fall

Words and Music by
John Denver, Mike Taylor and Dick Kniss

win-ter's on its way, ____ I close my eyes ____ re-mem-ber-ing the warmth ____

____ of yes-ter-day. ____ It seems a shame ____ to see Sep - tem - ber ____

____ swal-lowed by the wind ____ and more than that it's oh ____ so ____ sad ____

____ to see ____ the sum-mer end. And though ____ the chang-ing col-ors ____ are a

love-ly thing— to see,———— if it were mine to make— a change,— I

think I'd let it be. ——————————————— But I

don't re-mem-ber hear- ing—an-y-bod - y ask-ing me. ——————

Winter

Words by John Denver
Music by John Denver, Mike Taylor and Dick Kniss

And oh,_____ I must be get-ting old - er

and all this snow is try'n'___ to get___ me down.__

There's a fire_____ in the cor - ner slow - ly

dy - ing,_____ some-times I just don't feel like go - in' on,__

And yet I know it's more___ than worth the

wait - ing _____ for an - oth-er chance___ to see the sum - mer sun.___

Come on shine on me!___

There's a fire__ see the sum - mer sun.__

Come on,__ shine on _____ me! _____

Late Winter, Early Spring
(When Everybody Goes To Mexico)

Words and Music by
John Denver, Mike Taylor and Dick Kniss

Spring

**Words and Music by
John Denver, Mike Taylor and Dick Kniss**

clear blue sky and bright-ly shin-ing sun._____

O - pen up__ your ears__ and hear__ the breeze - es say__

ev - 'ry - thing__ that's cold__ and gray is gone._____

O - pen up__ your hands__ and feel__ the rain__ come on down, taste the wind__

and smell the flow-ers' sweet per-fume.

O-pen up your mind and let the light shine in, the

earth has been re-born and life goes on. And

do you care what's hap-pen-ing a-round you?

of ev-'ry-thing__ is here__ in me._____ A part__

of ev-'ry-thing__ is here__ in me,_____ a part of ev -

-'ry-thing__ is here__ in me._____

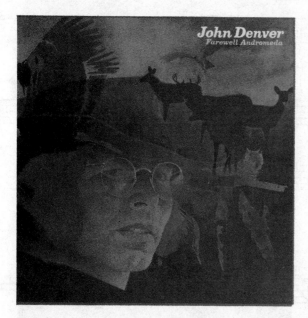

From the album
FAREWELL
ANDROMEDA

Release date: Summer 1973

I'D RATHER BE A COWBOY (Lady's Chains)

is another of my favorite songs. I became aware that there were many people involved in relationships in which the woman felt unfulfilled and had no opportunity to express herself. They needed to separate from the relationship in order to complete themselves as individuals. I pictured a couple living back in the woods or in the mountains in a very simplistic life, with perhaps not many friends and few opportunities to see a whole other side of the world. The woman decides to go to the city and wants her man to join her. He has decided that he'd rather be a cowboy; he'd rather live here in these mountains.

WELCOME TO MY MORNING (Farewell Andromeda)

is just a wonderful song of celebration. I had just finished the EST training and the song is dedicated to EST and to Werner Erhard. It has to do with taking responsibility for your life. You make the day the way it is, especially in your mind. I love the song in concert and as an introduction to an album. What I am doing is bringing you into my life and bringing you into my views, my experiences and I welcome you to that. I want you to know that I'm responsible right here and now for whatever it is that I might be doing. Welcome to my morning.

I'd Rather Be A Cowboy (Lady's Chains)

Words and Music by
John Denver

*Guitarists: Tune sixth string down to D.

rath-er be a cow-boy, I think I'd

rath-er ride the range,

I think I'd rath-er be a cow-boy than to

lay me down in love and la-dy's chains.

Tacet

I'd rath-er live ___ on ___ the side ___ of a moun-tain than ___

wan-der ___ through can-yons ___ of con - crete ___ and steel, ___

I'd rath-er laugh ___ with the rain ___ and sun -

shine and lay ___ down ___ my sun-down ___ in some star-ry ___

field. _____

Oh, but I miss her in the morn - in' when I a - wake__ a - lone,__ and the ab - sence of her laugh - ter is a cold and emp - ty sound.__ But her mem - o - ry al - ways makes__ me smile____ and

136

I think I'd rath-er be ___ a cow - boy ___ than to

lay me down ___ in love ___ and la-dy's chains.

and la-dy's ___ chains. ___

Welcome To My Morning
(Farewell Andromeda)

Words and Music by
John Denver

Brightly

1.3. Wel-come to my morn - in',___ wel-come to my__ day,___ oh, yes,
2. Wel-come to my hap - piness, you know it makes me__ smile,___ and it

I'm the one__ re-spon - si - ble, I made it just__ this way to make__
pleas-es me__ to have__ you here For just a lit - tle while, while__ we o -

__ my - self some pic - tures,__ see what they__ might__ bring.__ I
-pen up the spac-es__ and try to break__ some__ chains.__ And

Rocky Mountain Suite
(Cold Nights In Canada)

Words and Music by
John Denver

Zachary And Jennifer

Words and Music by
John Denver

ev - er, in this mir-ror see — to - mor-row, all the

joy and — all ____ the sor-row we can on — ly hope — to

share.

From the album
BACK HOME AGAIN

Release date: 1974

BACK HOME AGAIN has to do with spending so much time on the road. I remember coming home one day and sitting up in my loft watching a storm coming across the valley, hearing Annie working down in the kitchen and feeling so good about being home. I thought what it must be like for many people and tried to apply it to my situation, and then say how wonderful it is to be back home again and experience all the things that you feel, the little things that represent home, that nothing out there on the road could replace.

THIS OLD GUITAR was written about the guitar that my grandmother gave me when I was twelve years old—an old beat-up f-hole Gibson. What an incredible influence it has had on my life. What I did was sit down and in about three minutes, told my life story. It's all in the song, simply in the song.

ANNIE'S SONG, I'm continually learning, is my most famous song. It was written one day when Annie and I had been going through some difficult times, and we were back together again. We really felt together and much closer from the experiences we'd been through. One day I was skiing and I had just finished a run and was totally exhilerated. It was an incredible physical thing that I had just done, and I skied right down to the lift and got right on a chair and was off and up the mountain again, still in the process of catching my breath. I looked out on the mountains and the Colorado sky was a blue color that you can only see up here in the Rocky Mountains. The deep green of the evergreen trees, the snow and the beautiful ski outfits the people were wearing, the sounds of the lift as it goes over each tower, and people going down the slope laughing and joking and the smells out there in the wilderness—all these things were going through my mind and filling up my senses. I began thinking about other things that are like that for me. My first thought was of Annie and how she fills me so completely. Then I started thinking of other things in nature. In the ten minutes it takes to go from the bottom of the Bell Mountain lift to the top, I had written *Annie's Song*. I had the melody in my head, and I know the chords on the guitar. I skied down to the bottom of the hill, raced home, picked up my guitar and played it. I'm grateful to Annie and I'm grateful for the song. It's great to sing it now, because I can sing it not only to Annie, but I sing it to everybody. I sing it to people—to them, not just for them, but to them, to let them know that they too fill me. Life fills me.

COOL 'AN GREEN 'AN SHADY started off as a little

exercise on the guitar—the notion of boy, wouldn't it be nice to just sit down and relax, to lay down under a tree someplace in the shade on a hot day. I wrote that song with my friend, Joe Henry. It's that laid-back feeling when you want to lay down and take a nap under a tree.

MATTHEW was written for my father's family. My grandfather Deutschendorf

came to the United States when he was twelve years old. He was with his aunt from Germany, settled in Oklahoma and raised a family there—a family of eleven children. They grew up during the depression years, a very difficult time. The thing that I remembered most in our visits to the Deutschendorf farm was the celebration in the work they did; hard work with their hands, with the land. The epitomy of that was my Uncle Dean who was the second youngest of Dad's brothers. I went on my first wheat harvest with Dean. He was killed in a car accident, and one day, thinking about him and the family, I wrote the song *Matthew,* another one of my very favorites.

THE MUSIC IS YOU is just a little poem I put together one day.

People have written to me about the magic they hear in my music sometimes. I have a feeling that I'm very lucky in my life to find these songs, but as I said earlier, the music is out there. I just happen to be the guy listening when that particular song floated by that day. It's your music. I'm more a vehicle or a tool for putting it down, but it's your music. So, you know what music does for me, that it makes pictures, it tells stories. It's all there, but the music is you, the magic is you.

ECLIPSE was written when I was out in California doing the McCloud Show. I

played Dewey Cobb, a young deputy sheriff from Colorado. I was staying at the Universal Sheraton Hotel out by the Universal Studios where most of the filming was done. One night, I was sitting in my room, playing the guitar and I looked across toward Burbank. The sun was going down in the West and the moon was coming up in the East. It seemed like there was a shadow on it. I wrote the song about the sadness of being in the city for a long time, caught up in the smog and not being able to see the mountains. The shaded moon hanging up there in the sky watching us for so long—I wonder what it thinks? How much is it seeing?

SWEET SURRENDER was written for a Walt Disney movie called

THE BEARS AND I. It is about a young Viet Nam veteran coming back from the war and going up in the Northwoods to settle some things for his father and for a friend who had been in the Marines with him and had been killed. He didn't know what he wanted to do, and he was taking some time off by himself to go honor a last request of his friend. So, the first part of the song talks about not knowing what the future holds and yet, not being in a hurry to get there. Then, the song moves to the idea of surrendering to life. I believe we are all on the same path. It takes many different forms, is found in many different places, but we're all on the same path. Joy, really, is in surrendering to what life has to offer. So surrender—not without purpose. It's not giving up or succumbing—it's taking steps yourself, it's moving forward and not sitting around and waiting for something to happen. Don't hold back because you're afraid of something. Surrender—go for it and surrender.

This Old Guitar

Words and Music by
John Denver

love-ly place_ and a love-ly space_ to be._

I love__ to sing my songs_ for you, Yes, I do,_ you know,_

And I love_ to sing_ my songs_ for you._

Repeat and fade

Annie's Song

Words and Music by
John Denver

158

Grandma's Feather Bed

Words and Music by
Jim Connor

Chorus

Well, I love my Ma, I love my Pa,— I love Gran-ny and Grand-pa too, I been fish-in' with my un-cle, I ras-sled with my cou-sin, I e-ven kissed— Aunt Lou ooo! But if I ev-er had— to make a choice, I guess it ought-a be

Back Home Again

Words and Music by
John Denver

mile   or more a - way, ___   The whin-in' of ___ his wheels ___

___   just makes it   cold - er. ___   He's an

hour   a - way   from   rid - in' ___   on your prayers   up   in   the
all   the news   to   tell him: ___   just   how'd   you spend your
sweet - est thing   I   know of, ___   just spend - in' time with

sky;   And ten days   on ___   the road ___   are bare - ly
time?   And what's the lat - est thing ___   the neigh-bors
you,   It's the lit - tle things ___ that make ___   a house a

Some-times__ this old farm__ feels__ like a long-lost

friend. Yes 'n' hey, it's good__ to be back home a-gain.

1. **2.**

There's

And oh, the time that

I can lay__ this tired__ old bod-y down and

168

feel your fin - gers feath - er soft up - on me.

The kiss - es _____ that I live for, _____ the

love that lights my way, _____ The hap-pi - ness _____ that

D.S. 𝄋
and fade
on Chorus

liv - in' with you brings me. _____ It's the

Matthew

Words and Music by
John Denver

He was his moth-er's pride and joy. Yes, and

joy was just a thing that he was raised on

Love was just a way to live and die

Gold was just a wind-y Kan-sas wheat-field

Blue was just the Kan-sas sum-mer sky.

Last time to Coda

All the sto - ries that he told me
Well, I guess_ there were some hard times
And so he came_ to live at our house

Back when I was just a lad
And I'm told some years were lean
And he came to work the land

All the mem-'ries that he gave me
They had a storm in 'for - ty sev - en
He came to ease my dad - dy's bur - den

All the good times that_ he had.
A twist - er came and stripped_ 'em clean.
And he came to be_ my friend.

174

Thank God I'm A Country Boy

Words and Music by
John Martin Sommers

Moderately

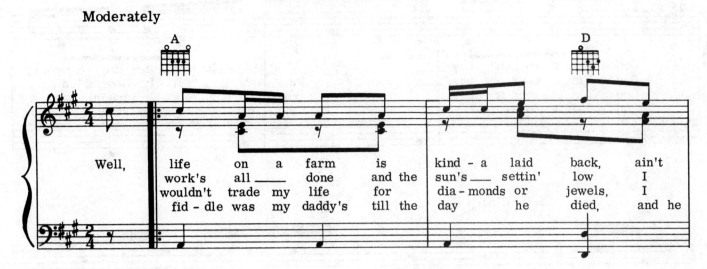

Well, life on a farm is kind-a laid back, ain't
work's all ___ done and the sun's ___ settin' low I
wouldn't trade my life for dia-monds or jewels, I
fid-dle was my daddy's till the day he died, and he

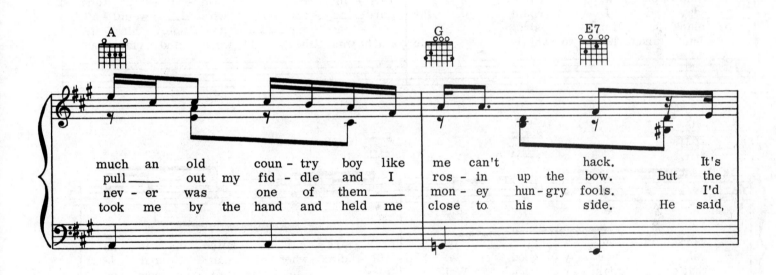

much an old coun-try boy like me can't hack. It's
pull ___ out my fid-dle and I ros-in up the bow. But the
nev-er was one of them ___ mon-ey hun-gry fools. But the I'd
took me by the hand and held me close to his side. He said,

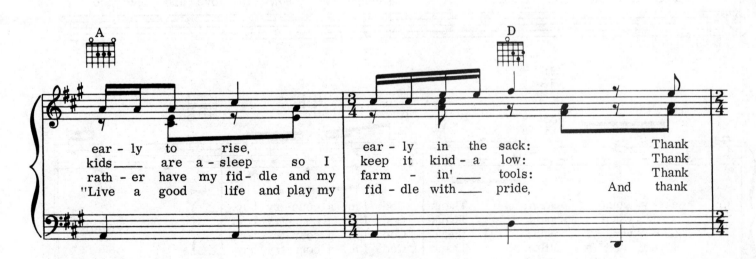

ear-ly to rise, ear-ly in the sack: Thank
kids ___ are a-sleep so I keep it kind-a low: Thank
rath-er have my fid-dle and my farm-in' ___ tools: Thank
"Live a good life and play my fid-dle with ___ pride, And thank

got me a fine wife, I got me old fid-dle. When the

sun's com-in' up I got cakes on the grid-dle; And

life ain't noth-in' but a fun-ny, fun-ny rid-dle:____ Thank

(4th time only)

(4th time)

God I'm a coun-try boy.____

1. 2. 3.

2. When the
3. I
4. Well, my

4.

The Music Is You

Words and Music by
John Denver

Moderately

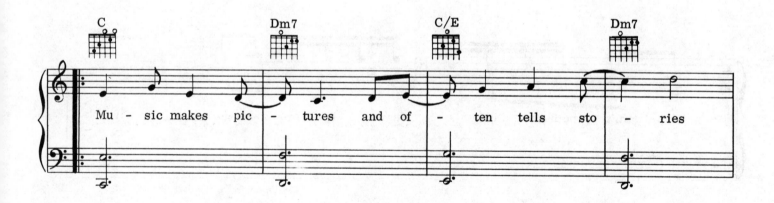

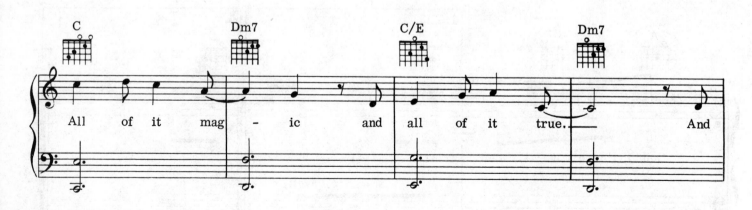

Mu - sic makes pic - tures and of - ten tells sto - ries

All of it mag - ic and all of it true. And

all of the pic - tures and all of the sto - ries And all of the mag - ic, the mu - sic is you.

After repeat, D. C. and fade

179

Eclipse

Words and Music by
John Denver

Moderately

The

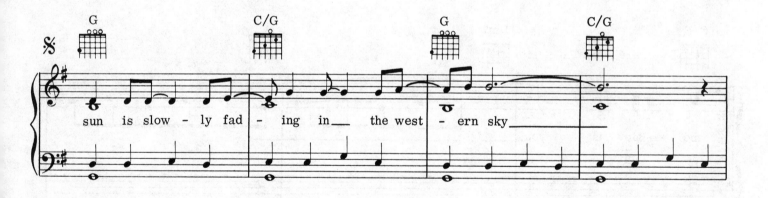

sun is slow-ly fad-ing in___ the west-ern sky___

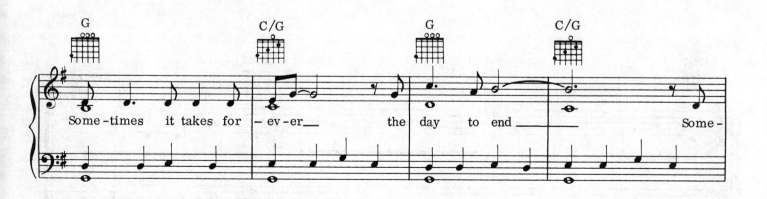

Some-times it takes for-ev-er___ the day to end___ Some-

183

Sweet Surrender

Words and Music by
John Denver

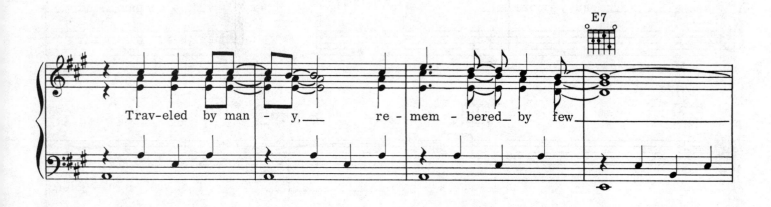

day,_____ And I don't know_____ what the fu - ture_____ is hold-in' in

store_____ I don't know where I'm go-in', I'm_____ not sure_____ where I've

been._____ There's a spir - it that guides_____ me, a

light that shines for me_____ My life is worth the liv - in', I don't

need to see the end._____

Cool An' Green An' Shady

Words by John Denver and Joe Henry
Music by John Denver

From the album WINDSONG

Release date: Fall 1975

I'M SORRY looks at women and an aspect of their lives that was becoming more and more prevalent at the time the song was written. They were finding that they weren't happy in their relationships with their men and with their children-they felt stifled. All of a sudden, within the women's liberation movement, they began to find the courage to say—Well, maybe I don't have to be stuck here, and I'm going to take a step and go out and make a different and perhaps better life for myself. It was kind of a new thing, and I thought about what it must be like to be the man in that situation, with or without children, when the woman really wants to take a break and get away to make her own life. All of a sudden it came down to the fact that if she left, he is forced to look at some things that he didn't take seriously before. Now, in his pain about all of the things that built up to this particular event, he's sorry for everything, for the times he didn't listen, sorry for the things he did or didn't say, but mostly sorry for himself. When you're sorry, generally you're sorry for yourself most of all.

CALYPSO was written for my friend, Captain Jacques Cousteau, a wonderful man—and not just for him, but for the crew of the Calypso. I had the pleasure of being with Captain Cousteau as part of a television special for ABC. The day I got on the boat, in the afternoon, just walking around on deck, I had the chorus to the song. It was a sea shanty and it had a lot of spirit and life to it—a celebration for what those guys are doing. Then, I began struggling with the verses, wanting to get them done in time for the show. I couldn't get them completed. It just killed me not to have it done. Finally one day, I just gave up and went skiing. The pressure was off after a couple of runs and I had let go of the song. But then, I felt the need to get back to it, so I jumped in the car and in the twenty minutes it took to get home I had worked out the verses. This is an example that I use when I tell people about being the instrument of that which wants to be written. Sometimes what you have to do is get yourself, your ego, out of the way and just let it happen. This was my experience with *Calypso* and it's one of my favorites. Generally, I close concerts with it. It's a song of celebration and speaks of a commitment to make a contribution to life and to the quality of life on this planet. I also feel that commitment, that kind of ideal and purpose in what I do with my music.

FLY AWAY was written about someone whose life just hasn't come together—a person who is living in a space of unhappiness, unfulfillment and dissatisfaction; wishing and dreaming of having a lover; dreaming of having children, but never willing to take responsibility and go out and make it happen. So, within the fantasy, she always flys away—her mind flies away but she never does anything about it. Again, the song says it for me.

LOVE IS EVERYWHERE was written with Joe Henry, John Sommers and Steve Weisberg. John Sommers had written a lovely chorus and I wanted to write words to it. I wanted to write a modern blue-grass song. John and I worked out the chorus, then John, Steve and I spent some time trying to get verses for the song, but we just couldn't get it the way I wanted it. So, I brought Joe Henry in and he worked some with John and Steve, but again, nothing much came of it. One night, after all the discussion, the talking, the approach and the critique, we were in the studio recording the *Windsong* album, Joe went home and virtually wrote the verses to the song. It was on my insistence that we shared credit all around because I think the song came out of all those discussions and interchange of ideas.

LOOKING FOR SPACE resulted from my experience in the EST training. EST is an educational corporation founded by Werner Erhard, a dear friend and wonderful man. EST has its own jargon, its own vocabulary if you will, and I know it sometimes drives people crazy. What they talk about is space; the space you create, the space you live in, the environment you live in, you create for yourself. It speaks of space in a much different way than that which is out there in the vacuum we perceive when we look into the heavens. I was looking to find out what my space is, what the area is that I occupy and what space my ideas, my intentions and my purposes are in. I believe that for all of us, one of the purposes of life, one of the processes of life is to find, to create, to determine and to define our own space. It's always there—it's never not there, but it takes time to see it or to feel it or to be able to communicate about it. Looking for space on the road of experience, day to day experience, looking for space.

WINDSONG My friend Joe Henry and I were talking one night about the wind, and I told him that I wanted to write a song about the wind. We discussed all of our feelings about it. We talked about many of the things that are in the song; how it touches everything, it passes over, it doesn't question, it doesn't wonder, it makes no judgement, but sees everything and touches everything. I went to bed and Joe went up to the loft. The next morning when I got up, he had written down the words to *Windsong*. I changed a couple of words and then wrote music to it but the song really came from both of us.

SHIPMATES AND CHEYENNE brought Joe Henry and I together for the first time at a concert in Tuscon, Arizona. Joe had really identified with some of the songs I'd written for earlier albums, and wanted to give me some material he thought I might be interested in. One of the things was the poem, *Shipmates and Cheyenne*. I really loved the poem, and it was about three or four years after that when I finally wrote the music to it. His poem, his words, my music.

SPIRIT

I'm an amateur astronomer, and I was up one night showing Joe Henry the stars through my telescope—pointing out Hercules and Vega, the second brightest star in the sky, which is in the constellation of Lyra. Lyra is the harp. There's the story of how Apollo visited an earthly maiden, and the fruit of their time together was a fellow named Orpheus. Although he was the son of a mortal woman and an immortal father, he was mortal. He was a musician, playing the harp and singing. It was said in those times that the greatest thing that could happen to a mortal was that when he died—if he had made an incredible contribution to humanity—they would take whatever it was that symbolized his life on earth and throw it up into the heavens as a constellation and that became his immortality. When Orpheus died, his father, Apollo, the god of poetry and music, came down and took his harp and threw it up into the heavens. That's the constellation you see today. There's a ring nebulla in Lyra which looks like a tiny smoke ring. It's a beautiful thing to see in the sky. I fantasize that I used to live in the ring nebulla in Lyra. Maybe I used to be Orpheus—who knows? So, there's a lot of fantasy in the song, in the stars and in the spirit that lives eternally. That night Joe stayed up in the loft and wrote the lyrics to *Spirit* and I checked on it the next day. We changed a few things, then I wrote the music. What a wonderful song.

Windsong

Words and Music by
John Denver and Joe Henry

wind watch-es o-ver our strug-gles and pleas-ures, The wind is the god-dess who
wind is the tak-er and giv-er of morn-ings, The wind is the sym-bol of

D   A7

first learned to fly.
all that is free.

The
So

D

wind is the bear-er of bad and good tid-ings The weav-er of dark-ness, The
wel-come the wind and the wis-dom she of-fers The Fol-low her sum-mons when

G

bring-er of dawn   The wind gives the rain, Then
she calls a - gain,   In your heart and your spir-it let the

builds us a rain - bow, The wind is the sing - er who
breez - es sur - round you, Lift up your voice then and

To Coda ⊕

sang the first song._____ The
sing with the first wind._____ La

wind is a twist - er of an - ger and warn - ing, The

wind brings the frag - rance of fresh - ly mown hay, The

wind is a rac-er and a white stal-lion run-ning And the sweet taste of love on a

D. S. al Coda 𝄋

slow sum-mer's day. The

Coda

la la la la_ la la_ la la la la la_ la la,

Dee dee dee dee_ dee dee dee_ ooo_

decresc.

Spirit

Words by Joe Henry
Music by John Denver

*Recorded in A♭ major

D. S. al Coda

3. His

Coda

fill.

Love Is Everywhere

Words by John Denver, Joe Henry,
Steve Weisberg and John Martin Sommers
Music by John Martin Sommers

O- pen your eyes to the joy and pain.
Sweet wa - ter run-ning to the cold salt sea.

Life is the fruit of your
Old man moon on a

own cre - a - tion,
white - top moun - tain,

Ev - 'ry new birth is a
Sound of the wind sing - in'

soul re -
dreams for

*After repeat
D. S. al Coda*

gained.
me.

Coda

me.

Shipmates And Cheyenne

Words by Joe Henry
Music by John Denver

* Tune lowest string to D.

Coda

I'll hold me one, one more ris - ing

sun   Till my day - light and dark - ness is done.

Hmm

Ooo

Ooo

Looking For Space

Words and Music by
John Denver

I'm Sorry

Words and Music by
John Denver

what they used to be,
things I did-n't say,
chains I put on you,

But
But
But

more than an-y-thing else
more than an-y-thing else
more than an-y-thing else

I'm sor-ry for my-self
I'm sor-ry for my-self
I'm sor-ry for my-self

'Cause you're not here
I can't be-lieve you
For liv-in' with-out

with me.
went a-way.
you.

1.

2. 3.

2. Our

Fly Away

Words and Music by
John Denver

She's

Calypso

**Words and Music by
John Denver**

sail on a dream on a crys-tal clear o-cean, To ride on the crest of the
dol-phin who guides you, You bring us be-side you To light up the dark-ness and

wild rag-ing storm, To work in the ser-vice of
show us the way. For though we are stran-gers in

life and the liv – ing, In search of the an – swers to ques – tions un –
your si – lent world,___ To live on the land we must learn from the

known___
sea,___

To be part of the move – ment and
To be true as the tide___ And

part of the grow – ing
free as a wind – swell,

Part of be – gin – ning
Joy – ful and lov – ing in

to un – der –
let – ting it

stand.___
be.

ff Aye,___ Ca – lyp – so, The

plac-es you've been to, The things that you've shown us, The sto-ries you tell!

Aye,___ Ca-lyp-so, I sing to your spi-rit, The men who have served you so

long and so well. Hi-dee – ay – ee – ooo_____ do-dle-

oh – ooo do do do do do do-dle-ay – ee

do-dle - ay - ee.

D.S. al Coda 𝄋

Like the

From the album
ROCKY MOUNTAIN CHRISTMAS

Release date: Winter 1975

A BABY JUST LIKE YOU

was written at the request of Frank Sinatra. His daughter Nancy had given birth to a daughter named Angela. With the birth of his first grandchild, Frank's whole sense of life and its meaning seemed to transform. Things that were old and taken for granted were brand new again, in the life of this little baby. He asked me to write a Christmas song about that. Once again, I sat down with Joe Henry and we talked it over. We talked about what it must be like for somebody to have seen everything in life, to have done it all, to have perhaps gotten to the point where life was a little too cold and where things had lost their meaning. Then, to have something like this happen and to relate it to that specific event almost 2,000 years ago when a baby was born, created in the image of God. To bring those two things together in this song was a magical experience.

Christmas For Cowboys

Words and Music by
Steve Weisberg

wind sings a hymn as we bow down to pray, It's
So man-y gifts have been o-pened to day, —

1.
Christ-mas for cow-boys and wide o-pen plains. It's

2.
Ours is the sky

— and the wide o-pen range, It's Christ-mas for cow-boys and

wide o-pen plains.

rit.

233

A Baby Just Like You

Words and Music by
John Denver and Joe Henry

From the album SPIRIT

Release date: Summer 1976

WRANGELL MOUNTAIN SONG is a song that

evolved from my experience up in Alaska. I discovered a place called McCarthy and a group of mountains called the Wrangell Mountains. It was like I had lived there before. That's the first time I've been anyplace that felt as comfortable to me as the Rockies. My time in Alaska was spent with bush pilots and I put together this story about a guy just back from Viet Nam who is living in Alaska on the frontier, and wants to build a cabin with his lady and lead a basically simple life as a bush pilot. One day he's trying to make it home in his plane, flying the way bush pilots do, and it's a complete white-out. He has to follow the shoreline of the ocean where there's a little break in the ice. He's flying about fifty to one hundred feet off the ground and doing everything he can to make it home. It's a perfect scenario to me.

IT MAKES ME GIGGLE is, to me, a very funny song. It describes

those times when you kind of bubble over a little bit. Something happens and you just have to laugh, like watching your kids. It also says that the simple things in life are really the most meaningful to me. It's those things that give me this nice, enthusiastic sense of life which is sometimes expressed with a giggle.

PEGASUS is another song about growing up. It's told from the point of view

of a guy who somehow draws children to him. They're always around asking him to tell stories, some of which are true, some of which are fantasies. The song shows the relationship between a grown man and the little children who come to listen to his stories. He tries to share with them both the things he has found in life, as well as those things that he has lost.

THE WINGS THAT FLY US HOME Joe Henry is pri-

marily responsible for the words—I may have added one or two—and I wrote the music. If I remember correctly, Joe wrote that song for me about our relationship. It expresses the truth about the way we look at things; how we sometimes color things depending on our individual positions and priorities in life. The real truth, though, is the spirit that is in all of us. We are all one, we are all brothers and sisters and it is that spirit which brought us into the world and that which will take us from this world to our home in heaven.

Wrangell Mountain Song

Words and Music by
John Denver

to see___ the Wran - gell Moun - tains.___ I can't wait___

to do___ what I___ will do.___

Hon - ey, did I nev - er say___ how time___ goes by so___ slow - ly___ When I

can't wait___ to get back home___ to you.___ It's a qui-

It Makes Me Giggle

Words and Music by
John Denver

Baby, You Look Good To Me Tonight

Words and Music by
Bill Danoff

feet are mov-ing slow_____ I've got to stop and eat_____
brought it on_ a tray_____ She said, "It would be nice

_____ While it's still light_____ There's a lo-cal an-gel
_____ if you could stay, _____ You're the best_ i-

sit-ting on my_____ right_____ Do you be-lieve in
dea I've had all_ day,_____ _ U-su-al-ly

love at_ first_ sight?_____ _ Ba-by, you_ look
I put up a_ fight_____ but Ba-by, you_ look

good to me— to-night—
good to me— to-night."—
Well, I'm
Well, I'm

or-din-a—ri-ly ver-y shy— And I'd be po-lite— if I
or-din-a—ri-ly ver-y shy— But I grinned at her— as I

had the time— Ba-by, you look good— to me— to-night—
ate my pie— Said, ba-by, you look good— to me— to-night—

To-mor-row I'll be good and gone—
I thought I must be in a dream— When she

des - ti - ny's your own, You go as far as you can go_____ And if there's time to sleep_____

There's time to make_____ love_____

Like A Sad Song

Words and Music by
John Denver

Some-times I feel like a sad song _____ Like I'm

all a-lone ____ with-out you. 2. So you.

I know that life goes on just per-fect-ly _____ And

ev-'ry-thing ____ is just the way _____ that it should be

Still there are times when my heart feels like break-ing_____ And

an-y-where___ is where___ I'd rath-er be

Oh, and in the night-time_____ I know that it's the right time___ To hold_

___ you close and say I love you so To

Ooo

Some-times I feel   like a

sad song,___   Like I'm   all a-lone___   with-out   you,   with-out

you.

Pegasus

Words by Joe Henry
Music by John Denver

End - less hall - ways dark with sleep and __ riv - ers dark with sound __
nev - er tell __ your se - cret cross my heart and hope to die __

Peace - ful val - leys, an - i - mals __ and chil - dren ask - ing me

Tell me sto - ry that __ you told __ of sail - ors drink - ing tea __

Tell the one __ a - bout __ the man __ who sad - dled up the wind __

Peg-a-sus and fly-ing fish and wood-men made of tin___

1.

Peg-a-sus and fly-ing fish and wood-men made of tin___

2.

Peg-a-sus and fly-ing fish and wood-men made of tin___

rit.

The Wings That Fly Us Home

Words by Joe Henry
Music by John Denver

dreamed I was a moun-tain in__ the wind I

dreamed you knelt and touched me with a flow-er__

I a-woke with this: a flow-er__ in my

hand I know that love__ is see-ing__ all the

Come And Let Me Look Into Your Eyes

Words and Music by
John Denver and Joe Henry

wis-dom____ is-n't un-der-ground____ Nor on a moun-tain side____

And where am I____ to take____ my-self____ There's

277

From the album
I WANT TO LIVE

Release date: 1977

I WANT TO LIVE

resulted from my involvement with the Hunger Project and more expressly, out of my interest in what's going on with hunger in the world. It also came out of my involvement with the Presidential Commission on World and Domestic Hunger as well as my feelings about the great whales, the dolphins, and other aspects of what I consider to be intelligent life on this planet. For all human beings, no matter who you are, the color of your skin, the philosophical, environmental or religious heritage you evolve from, that birth cry of a newborn infant is the same. It is the absolute desire and demand to live. The chorus, "I want to live, I want to grow, I want to see, I want to know, I want to share what I can give..." and I, each of us has something to give. It ought to be shared, it's what we in the world need from you. It is the most that you can give us. Having been born into this world, you have the right to live. Human rights are much more than just freedom of speech, freedom of press and religion. It is the right to breathe clean air; it is the right to drink and fill yourself, to cleanse yourself with clean water. It is a right that is denied millions of people today from before their birth. To me, that is the one obscenity in the world, and this song is a positive expression, a humanistic expression against that obscenity.

DRUTHERS

Sometimes I feel like I start taking life too seriously. I get involved in so many things. Sometimes, when I'm in Washington, D.C. or New York, or on the road somewhere and things are just weighing me down, I have these considerations about "I'd rather." What I'd rather be doing right now. If I had my "I'd rathers," which is druthers, I'd be fishing, or I'd be flying, or sailing, or perhaps skiing. You know?

HOW CAN I LEAVE YOU AGAIN

is another love song for Annie. I wrote it during Christmas a few years ago when I was involved in filming OH GOD. Having this project and a commitment to giving myself completely to that project was also a contradiction to the way I was feeling about myself and my life at the time; how much energy I was giving to my career, and to my professional life. It was keeping me from home, and around Christmas this is a very special time for our family—for any family. I really wanted to be there and be part of putting Christmas together—going out and getting our Christmas tree, helping decorate the house and welcoming the family. I got home at sunset on Christmas Eve and had to leave the morning after Christmas. As I was leaving, Annie was very sad—Christmas had not been that great for us that year. And I was sad, and here I was going off, and how can I leave you again, you know I just don't understand. At the same time I recognize that I made a choice a long time ago to give myself completely to life, and to take advantage of every opportunity I can to do the work I have to do to make my contribution in this world. I'm a sailor who runs to the sea.

SINGING SKIES AND DANCING WATERS

started off as a love song not only to Annie, not only to my children and an expression of my faith in my father in heaven and my earthly mother, but a love song for all people. I've gone through periods of knowing and not knowing, being up and being down, but if I just take the time to look a little bit past the problem facing me, I see the absolute joy and celebration that I find in every aspect of life. I see skies that sing to me and sunlight dancing on waters and children's faces full of laughter. I see you in that. This song is an expression of that love and that fulfillment which is always totally available to everyone.

TRADE WINDS

is another love song. Annie and I were down in the Bahamas for the first time, seeing a beautiful new part of the world-really enjoying laying back and being together. Here is a love song that comes out of a very specific kind of environment, a very specific kind of weather and a very specific kind of place. The music, the melody and the words are meant to alude to that particular situation, not here in the mountains but over there, on the ocean. I really enjoy it.

TO THE WILD COUNTRY

is an expression of the strong feeling I have for wilderness. I consider wilderness an invaluable resource that belongs to all the world regardless of which country or people or political elements is in control of the geography. The world's survival depends on the sharing and dispersing of those riches in an equitable manner so that all people can benefit from them.

IT AMAZES ME

is another autobiographical song. When I look around me, in search of answers to my questions about life, in moving, and growing, and discovering, I find that I am really amazed. I can't believe how magnificent people can be, and how inhumane at times. This is a transitional place. The most striking edifice we can build is a monument to man and will be dust someday. I rejoice in the way the world is made. I rejoice in the way life is.

I Want To Live

Words and Music by
John Denver

standing all to-geth-er face to face and arm in arm. We are standing on the thresh-hold of a dream, No more hun-ger, no more kill-ing, no more wast-ing life a-way; It is sim-ply an i-dea and I know its time has come. I want to

Druthers

Words and Music by
John Denver

Moderate country blues

mp

If I had my druth-ers I'd go fish-in',

Find my-self a lake and a la-zy day.

If I had my druth-ers I'd quit wish-in',

Look-in' for___ the things_ I'd like_ to see.___
Catch me camp-in' out___ on the o-pen sea.___

If I had___ my druth-ers I'd___ be try-in'_____ The
If I had___ my druth-ers I'd___ be sing-in'_____ A-

on-ly way___ to be what I can be. Give me
just how good___ this good life feels to me. You just

some-bod-y to love_ me, make me feel like the on-ly one,___ A-
need some-one___ to talk___ to,_____ some-thin' you can share.___ You don't

some - thin' that's worth do - in', Lord,___ I feel good when it's well done.
need no rea - son for liv - in', Lord,___ It's al - read - y there.___

(Spoken) I'm goin' fishin'

It Amazes Me

Words and Music by
John Denver

the wind will sure-ly some-day blow___ it all___ a-way.___ It a-maz-

-es___ me,___ And I'm___ so ver-y grate-ful that you made___ the world___ this

way.___

It a-maz-es,___ me,___ It a-maz-

-es me,___ It a-maz - es___ me.___

How Can I Leave You Again

Words and Music by
John Denver

pleas-ure I've gone where they go, In the qui - et still - ness

I can hear sym - pho - nies,__ the lov-li-est mu - sic I know.

Chorus

How can I leave_ you a - gain,__ I must be clear out of my mind,__

Lost in a storm_ I've gone blind,_____ Oh,

Singing Skies And Dancing Waters

Words and Music by
John Denver

To The Wild Country

**Words and Music by
John Denver**

Trade Winds

Words and Music by
John Denver

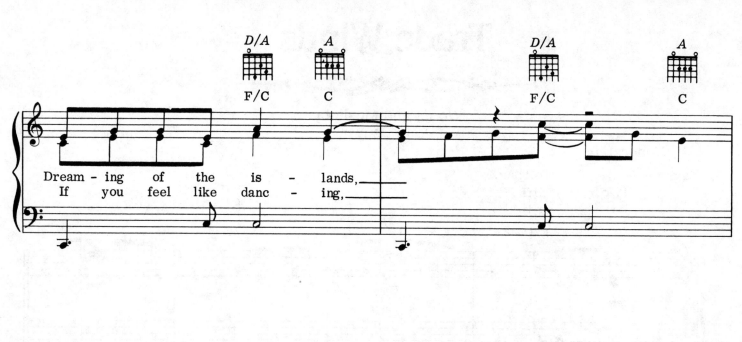

Dream - ing of the is - lands,
If you feel like danc - ing,

Wrap - ping my - self in a glow of the trop - i - cal moon,
Roll - ing like the wa - ter a - cross my sleep - less night,

I nev - er shiv - er when the sun goes down.
mak - ing me a peace - ful place.

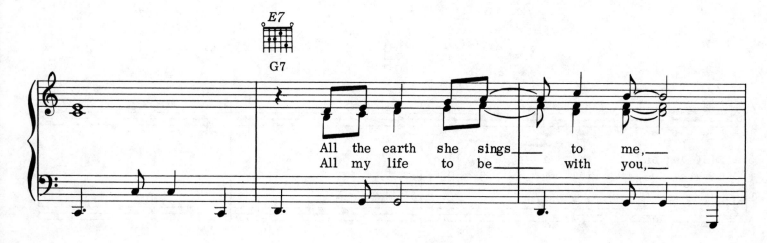

All the earth she sings to me,
All my life to be with you,

mem - o - ries,___ Sure -ly I was lost___ 'til I___ found these.___

Doo doo doo doo doo   doo___

Doo doo doo doo doo   doo___

Doo doo doo doo doo   doo___

Bet On The Blues

Words and Music by
Tom Paxton

You tell me you were a gam - b - lin' man,___

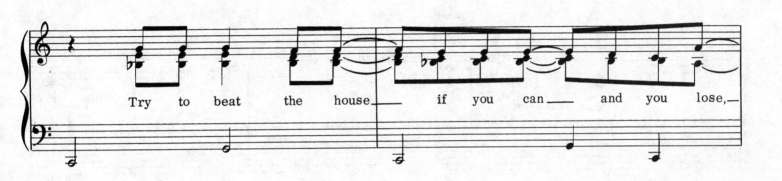

Try to beat the house___ if you can___ and you lose,___

F7

C7

Bet on the blues.___

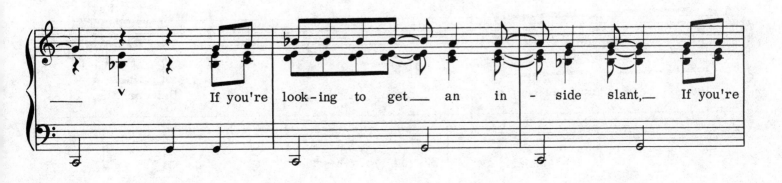

If you're look-ing to get___ an in - side slant,___ If you're

322

You say you found your la - dy fair,

Eight to five_ says she's wear - ing her trav - el - ing shoes,_

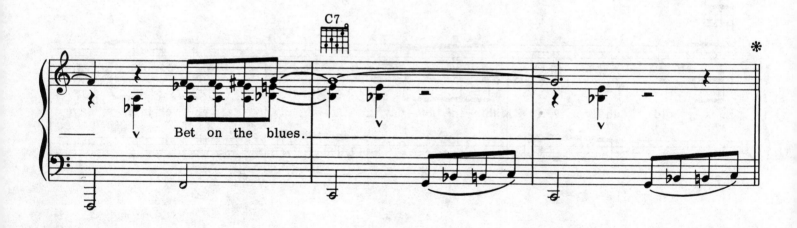

Bet on the blues.

*16 bar instrumental omitted here

Five hun-dred 'll buy___ you a stack,___ Bet it on___ the red___

___ or the black___ and you lose, Bet on the blues.___

If you're look-ing to get___ an in-

-side slant,___ If you're look-ing for some-thing so good___ you can't re-fuse,

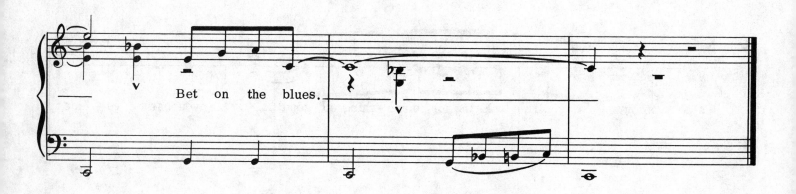

From the album JOHN DENVER

Release date: Winter 1979

DOWNHILL STUFF
I wanted to write a song about skiing. I had gone with a bunch of friends to Blue River, in Alberta, Canada. We were skiing out of the helicopter, skiing glaciers for five or six days in powder that's up to your waist and sometimes over your head. I wanted to write a song about it, but it rained most of the time we were up there. Then, I went on a camping trip the following summer, with about a 60-70 pound pack on my back, my guitar in my left hand and fishing rod in my right. It was about a seven mile hike to a particular lake we wanted to go to. All of the hike was up-hill. I realized very quickly that I had bitten off more than I could chew in regard to what I was carrying. The only way to stay with it was to put my mind elsewhere as I placed one foot in front of the other. What happened was *Downhill Stuff*. Some people like downhill stuff. Give me a break, Lord. I enjoy that song.

JOSEPH & JOE
has to do with two wonderful friends of mine. One of them is Joe Henry, who I've written so many songs with. Joe is a cowboy. Joe Frazier, who is Joseph in the song, is an old friend from the days in the Mitchell Trio. Now he's an Episcopalian priest. A few summers ago, Joseph and Joe both happened to show up in Aspen at the same time to visit with Annie and me. It was a wonderful little circle that we had together. The song came out of that circle—it's just a scenario. It also expresses the feeling that you can't go anyplace you haven't been to already, even in the sense that everything is new and there are so many places to go. If you picture it in your mind, or know of it, the truth is you're already there. You just have to take the physical steps to get there. You know everything. You just have to break down the barriers to your knowing—barriers that are in us because we are human beings; barriers implanted in us by our parents and our environment, and the world we live in. We have to break through all of that to get back to the truth, back to the center.

YOU'RE SO BEAUTIFUL
is another song that resulted from looking at my wife and my children, looking at the world, our beautiful mother Earth, and looking at the spirit of life and people everywhere. It really is a love song to all of that—to being alive, to sharing this life with you, to interacting with you.

LIFE IS SO GOOD
You know, life is good to me, and I don't know how to say it any better than that. Even at its worst, in those times when you look around and

cannot believe our inhumanity to each other, life is still so good. I look out on a day like this in Colorado. It snowed last night and none of it is melting. It's just as cold as it can be and . . . life is so good.

SONGS OF . . . is just a very simple expression about what all of my songs are. They are songs of the future; they are songs of the past, songs of the struggle, songs of the way . . . *Songs Of . . .* .

WHAT'S ON YOUR MIND is sitting there looking at somebody and not being able to say it. What you want to do is get really close, to make love and have it be all that it can be. You know, it's what I'm thinking about, but it's sometimes so difficult to say. The person who's sitting there with you, who is on your mind is probably thinking and feeling the same thing you are. How do you get it out to say it? I said it in a song.

What's On Your Mind

Words and Music by
John Denver

* Guitarists: Tune 6th string to D.

caught in the pass - ing of time. It's like too man - y miles,
too man - y heart-aches, too much that needs to be done, Yes, and
too man - y side - walks, too man - y peo - ple, too man - y hours a - lone.

Chorus

What's on your mind and what's on my mind

is real-ly quite the same, I've been work-ing so hard and I'm

read-y to play; I know just the right game.

What's on your mind is what's on my mind, that's the way it's gon-na be.

I'm gon-na find me a place I can hide;

During instrumental interlude, guitarists place capo across 2nd fret.

333

Chorus

335

Joseph & Joe

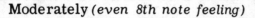

Words and Music by
John Denver

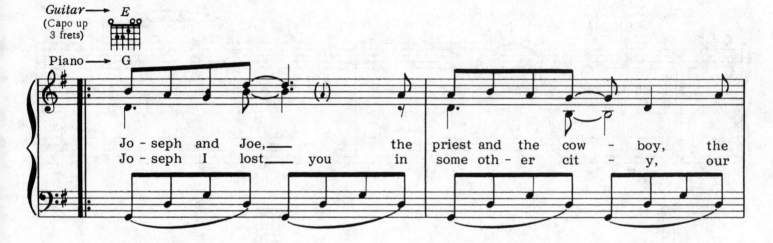

Jo - seph and Joe,___ the priest and the cow - boy, the
Jo - seph I lost___ you in some oth - er cit - y, our

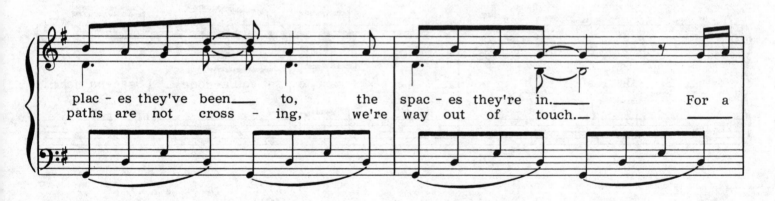

plac - es they've been___ to, the spac - es they're in.___ For a
paths are not cross - ing, we're way out of touch.___ ___

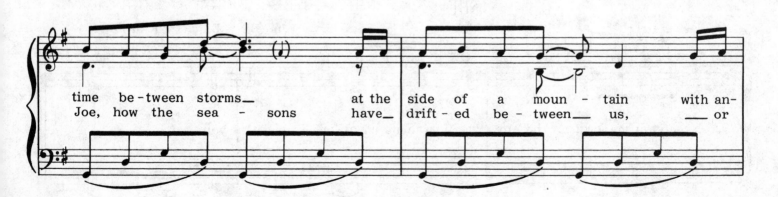

time be - tween storms___ at the side of a moun - tain with an -
Joe, how the sea - sons have___ drift - ed be - tween___ us, ___ or

oth - er man's fam - 'ly, ___ fam - 'ly and friends.
is it your vi - sion, much great - er than mine. ___

1. ___
2. Ooo ___
Jo-seph can give___ you the
Take heed of the dark - ness which

keys to the king-dom, ___ he'll put you in touch___ with the spi - rit of man. ___
gath-ers a-round us, ___ a fire that con - sumes___ us for - ev - er to burn.___ Then

Joe loves the des - ert but lives in the moun - tains, his clos - est com - pan - ion, a
look to the sun___ for our fa - ther is with___ us, our moth - er will teach___ us what

if you've nev-er___ nev-er___ been there?___ How do you know?___

Tell me how do you know.___

Tell me where do you go___ if you've

Downhill Stuff

Words and Music by
John Denver

Bright rock tempo

(Shouted) 1,   2,   3,   4

Some peo-ple like_ that down - hill_ stuff,_   they like it fast   and breez-

8va lower throughout

- y,   Some peo-ple walk_ on the oth - er side,   they

344

like it slow__ and eas - y.   Some peo-ple run__ on a moun-

- tain trail,__   some like it wild__ and rough.__

Some like to fly____ and   some like   to   sail,____ and

some like the down - hill__ stuff.__   There's

work in what__ we prac - tice,

work in the things__ we say.__

Some - times we work just to try to make a liv - ing, or we're

work-in' just to make it pay.__

Some - times we're try - in' to work__

__ our will,__ but that won't work__ an - y - way.__

like it slow__ and eas - y.   Some peo-ple run__ on a moun-

- tain trail,__   some like it wild__ and rough.__

Some like to fly____ and   some like   to sail,____   and

some like the down - hill__ stuff.____   Keep

*16 bar instrumental omitted.

Some like to fly___ and some like to sail,___ and some like the down-hill___ stuff,___

I like the down-hill stuff, Let me

slide down that down-hill stuff,___ Oh, hon-ey

give me that down-hill stuff.___

Life Is So Good

Words and Music by
John Denver

good,   life is so good these_ days,_ Life is so good these_ days,_ life is so

good.   Life is so good,   life is so good these_ days,_ life is so

good these days,_ life is so good.   *(Instrumental)*

Life is so

356

You're So Beautiful

Words and Music by
John Denver

Slowly, but not dragging

Lyrics:

Born on a qui-et morn-ing,___ Just a dream in some-one's eye,___ A dream that's like a prom-ise meant to be.___ Giv-ing rise to spec-u-la-tion___ On a place called par-a-dise;

* Originally recorded ½ step lower, in E major.

If I've ev-er been there it's when you were with me. You're so

beau - ti - ful, I can't be-lieve my eyes each time I see you a-gain.

You're so beau - ti - ful that

I'm in par-a-dise each time I see you a-gain. I re-

To Coda ⊕

358

Coda

And if par-a-dise___ is ev-'ry-thing___ you

see,___ Then the place you must___ be com-ing from___ is

ec - sta - cy.___ (remove capo) You're so

beau - ti - ful that I can't be-lieve___ my eyes___ each time___ I

360

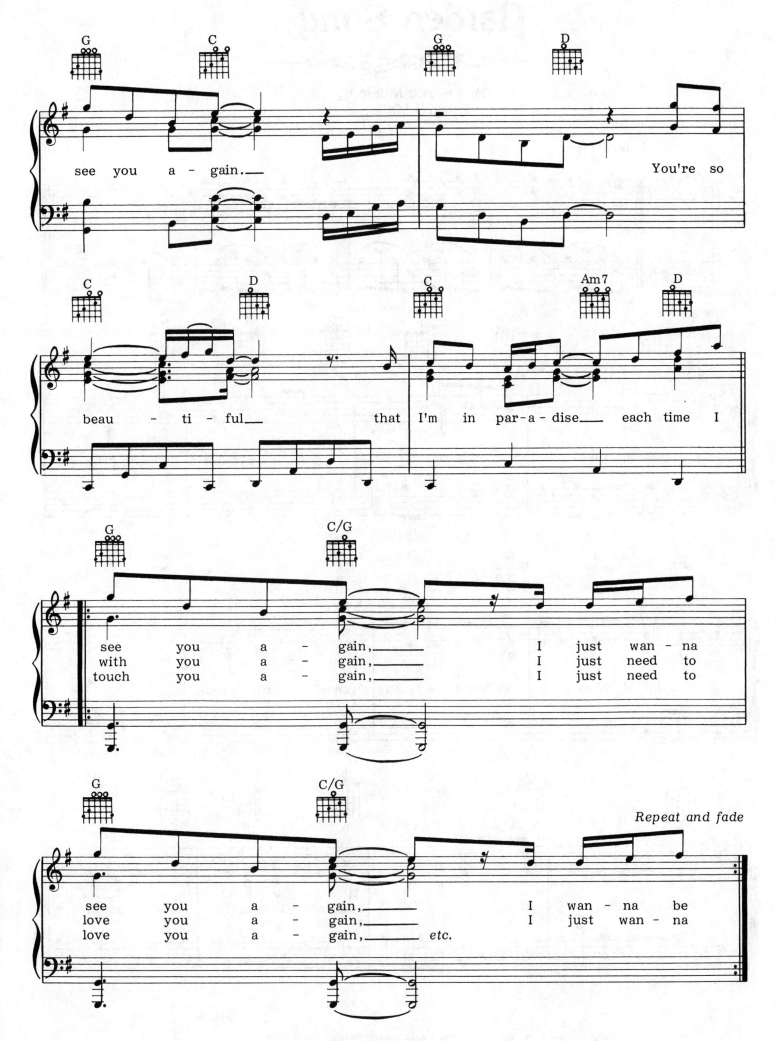

Garden Song

Words and Music by
David B. Mallett

Grain for grain, sun and_ rain,_ find my way in na-ture's chain,_

To my bod-y and my brain to the mu-sic from the land._

Songs Of . . .

**Words and Music by
John Denver**

In a slow 4 (♩.=1 beat)

(3 times)

D.S. and fade on Interlude 𝄋

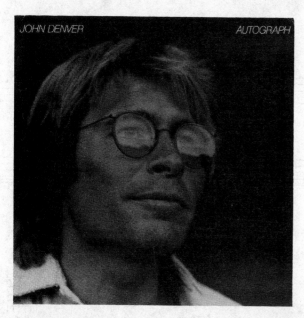

From the album AUTOGRAPH

Release date: Spring 1980

DANCING WITH THE MOUNTAINS
I got enamored with disco music. I'm really not a fan of disco to any great degree, and yet I see it as an incredible kind of energy and wanted to try and write a disco song. I really don't have the energy to spend on the dance floor, but, I see it as a wonderful exercise and opportunity for people to really express themselves. We are one when we are out there dancing; seeing, feeling and knowing together. When we think of each other we are one with each other.

AUTOGRAPH
I hate signing autographs. It is nothing more than a proof to somebody that they saw me in person. I can't think of anything less meaningful. What is meaningful is the music and how you feel about it—whether or not you get from my music the love that I feel from you. This is my autograph, this is what I want people to remember. Not my signature on a piece of paper, but this music, these songs and these feelings. This is the best that I have to give.

Dancing With The Mountains

Words and Music by
John Denver

*Guitarists: Tune 6th string to D

stretch your soul.___

Just re - lax___ and let the rhy - thm___ take___ you,
Were you___ there___ the night they lost the light - ning?

Don't you___ be - a - fraid to lose con - trol.___
Were you___ there___ the day the earth stood still?___

If your___ heart___ has found some
Did you___ see___ the fa - mous

emp - ty___ spa - ces,
and the___ fight - ing,

Danc - in's___ just___ a thing to make you whole.___
Did you___ hear___ the pro - phet tell his tale?___

G

D

I am one who danc - es with___ the moun - tains; _____
We are one, when danc - ing with___ the moun - tains, wo,

*Final fade omitted

You Say That The Battle Is Over

Words and Music by
David B. Mallett

3. Now the blame can-not fall ____ on the heads of a few, ____ It's be- come such a part of the race. ____ It's e- ter-nal-ly ____ trag - ic that that ____ which is mag - ic Be

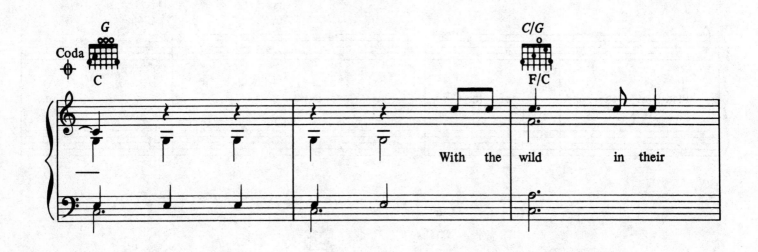

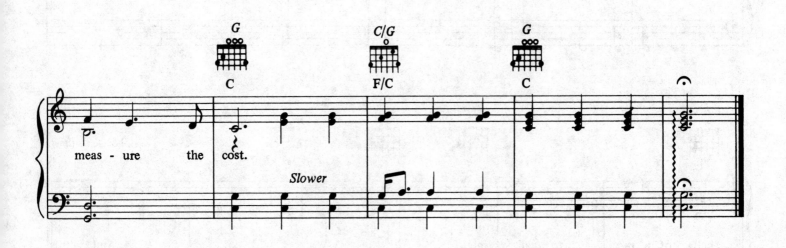

382

In My Heart

Words and Music by
John Denver

it is just ___ an il - lu - sion, it's not ___ e - ven real. ___

(It's) much more ___ than you think, ___ it's much more ___ than you

1.
feel. ___ My

2.
feel, ___ Do you

* 12 bar interlude omitted

Repeat and fade

feel. ___
feel ___ Is this real? ___ How I
heart... ___ *(continue instrumentally)* in my heart, ___ In my

American Child

Words by Joe Henry
Music by John Denver

Go - in' up to A - las - ka,   up to the land of the Mid - night

pic - ture the time___ when a man had to find___ his own way through an un - brok - en

land,_____ Be - fore the ma - chine changed the blue and the green to

some - thing you can't___ un - der - stand?___ A - mer - i - can Child, there's a

burn - ing in - side you that calls you a - way___ through the cold To

Whalebones & Crosses

Words by Joe Henry
Music by Lee Holdridge

Autograph

**Words and Music by
John Denver**

From the album SOME DAYS ARE DIAMONDS

Release date: 1981

COUNTRY LOVE
Words and Music by John Denver

Nashville tears are lonely signs
That point to broken hearts
Broken lives and families
That love has split apart
Children who miss daddy
Mommy's on the run
The pleasure that is painful
And hidden from the sun

Nashville hearts are lonely words
That speak of love gone wrong
Sad and soulful stories
And beautiful love songs
For each and every melody
Of happiness denied
You know that there's another one
That shows the other side

Country love is kisses in the kitchen
Country love is honest and it's true
Country love is home with your family
Country love's the way that I love you

Country love is silky nights
And warm familiar hands
Someone who's been there before
And always understands
Nashville nights are lonely roads
That we've all traveled on
Sometimes they take you far away
Or they can bring you home
If you're lost out on the highway
Do not deny the dove
When Nashville night's the question
The answer's country love

Country love is kisses in the kitchen
Country love is honest and it's true
Country love is home with your family
Country love's the way that I love you

SLEEPIN' ALONE
Words and Music by John Denver

For someone who's got everything
Life can still be rough
If things are what you're lookin' for
There's never quite enough
And all the tea in China
Won't make a house a home
You can be a millionaire
And still be sleepin' alone

There might be some one night stands
To ease the pain inside
Or someone you can call around
If you've lost all your pride
Please don't be mistaken
I don't mean to put that down
I know there's times when anything
Is better than sleepin' alone

Sleepin' alone can make a bottle
Just about your dearest friend
Sleepin' alone can make you swear to God
This night will never end

You know that it's not company
You are lookin' for
You know it's not just pleasure
You know it's somethin' more
You know it's not the answer
If it's not like comin' home
If the one who's there doesn't really care
It's worse than sleepin' alone

Sleepin alone can make a bottle
Just about your dearest friend
Sleepin' alone can make you swear to God
This night won't ever end

For someone who's got everything
Life can still be rough
If things are what you're lookin' for
There's never quite enough
And all the gold that glitters
Won't make a house a home
You can be a millionaire
And still be sleepin' alone
You might be a millionaire
And still be sleepin' alone

Country Love

Words and Music by
John Denver

Nash-

ville tears— are lone— ly signs— that point— to brok- en hearts,
Nash-ville hearts— are lone— ly words— that speak— of love— gone wrong,

Brok- en lives and fam - i - lies that love
Sad and soul - ful sto - ries and beau-

Coun - try love____ is silk - y nights____ and warm____ fa - mil - iar hands,____

Some-one who's been there____ be - fore____ and al-

ways un - der - stands,____

Coun - try love_ is home_ with your fam-'ly,_

Coun - try love's_ the way_ that I_ love you.

you.

411

Sleepin' Alone

Words and Music by
John Denver